BOSTON'S LOCKE-OBER CAFÉ

BOSTON'S LOCKE-OBER CAFÉ

An Illustrated Social History

With Miscellaneous Recipes

NED AND PAM BRADFORD

New York   Atheneum   1978

*The quotation on page 103, copyright © 1935
Ogden Nash, is from the collection
Verses from 1929 On.*

Library of Congress Cataloging in Publication Data

Bradford, Larned G
    Boston's Locke-Ober Café.

    1. Locke-Ober Café. I. Bradford, Pamela, joint author.
II. Title.
TX945.5.L56B7 1978   647'.95744'61   77–15871
ISBN 0–689–10865–6

FOR BILL AND KATE

A good restaurant is more or less like a good epic poem—it cannot be improved in a day. Tradition, knowledge, experience, and even genius, are necessary.

MAGNY

ACKNOWLEDGMENTS

Of all those who contributed to the making of this book, we are most indebted to William F. Harrington, a rich repository of Locke-Ober lore, whose original idea it was.

For material assistance in a variety of ways, we are also grateful to: Dean Lynch; Charles W. Little; Mrs. Marjorie Palmer, granddaughter of Frank Locke; Leon E. Ober, grandson of Louis Ober; Mrs. Laurette Wilson, granddaughter of Emil Camus; David Wells; Paul Queenan; and Mary Leen of the Bostonian Society.

ILLUSTRATIONS

Illustrations

BOSTON'S LOCKE-OBER CAFÉ

WHEN THE Civil War began, Boston was a thriving but more or less provincial town; when the war ended, it was a bustling metropolis with a new notion about what its future could be and a greater willingness to look toward Europe and the rest of the world for new ideas, new ways of living, new comforts, entertainments and satisfactions. To be sure, poverty and social inequity remained. The immigrants who had swarmed into the country in the forties and fifties continued to hew the wood and draw the water. They were still spiking the rails, driving the teams, manning the kitchens, minding the children in the New England social complex. But by and large the middle and upper classes had never lived better.

The war had, as all wars do, accelerated many processes. For one thing, manufacturing had grown tremendously in the space of a very few years. New textile mills, with their picturesque architectural embellishments, now lined many of the faster rivers. New England had become the major supplier of boots and shoes to the nation. Iron foundries were turning out firearms, agricultural implements, stoves and furnaces, engines, fences, pipes and hardware of every description. Canal boats and improved railroads were bringing more and more of the good things of America to Boston and, more dramatically, the magnificent wooden clipper ships and, later on, the iron-hulled steamers were carrying on a larger and larger trade with the Orient, the East Indies, West Indies and Europe—delivering exotic adornments for New England homes, interesting spices and condiments for New England tables.

The bankers, lawyers, insurers and financiers who lingered over their brandy and cigars at the Union Club, the Parker House or Locke-Ober's were as often as not arranging to underwrite a railroad or gold mine twenty-five hundred miles to the west. And as later historians have revealed, there was nothing ingenuous about their manipulations.

No society can of course boast of an uninterrupted progression from strength to strength. In 1872, Boston suffered its second great fire, which entirely devastated sixty acres of prime business and residential property in the heart of the city, causing total losses estimated at some $60,000,000, an almost unimaginable sum in those days and, incidentally, lapping at one of the entrances to Winter Place where Louis Philippe Ober was already operating a "cellar restaurant" and where his much expanded establishment would rise a short time later. The Panic of '73 would depress the American economy for five long years, although we may assume that it did not seriously tighten the purses of those to whom Mr. Ober's viands and bottled goods were meant to appeal. President Grant was nearing the end of a second undistinguished term, embarrassed, among other things, by the so-called Crédit Mobilier scandal in which various Boston railroad promoters were, almost inevitably, involved. But these were travails which Bostonians, and all Americans, had from considerable practice learned to live with. In spite of them, an unwavering

Louis Phillippe Ober—founder. His portrait, together with those of Frank Locke and Emil Camus, hangs in the second-floor bar.

belief in the inevitability of ultimate progress generally prevailed. Certainly economic conditions in the last three decades of the nineteenth century were such as to encourage the arts of life—the building and decorating of fine houses, the leisure and means to travel, the refinement of tastes in food and clothing, the patronage of the fine arts, the pursuit of culture which most people had been too preoccupied with survival to think a great deal about fifty years earlier. In the field of literature alone, the phrase "Athens of America" in reference to Boston and its institutions took on a genuine meaning. The intellectual climate was in fact charged with the work and reputations of such personages as Longfellow, Hawthorne, James Russell Lowell, Francis Parkman, Emerson, Louis Agassiz, Whittier, James Fields, William and Henry James, Edward Everett Hale, William Dean Howells, Oliver Wendell Holmes, Richard Henry Dana—many of whom, incidentally, were members of the famous Saturday Club which met at the Parker House and later at the Union Club once a month, except during the summer, when the members unabashedly celebrated each other at luncheons like this one given in honor of Holmes in 1870:

Littleneck Clams

Grilled Trout   Cucumbers, Sauteed

Omelette with Mushrooms in Cream   Grilled Plover

Filet Mignon   Potatoes   Asparagus with Hollandaise

Tomato and Lettuce Salad

Ice Cream   Strawberries   Cakes   Coffee

Nor was the Boston cultural scene uncongenial to talented outsiders. Howells, editor of *The Atlantic Monthly* from 1871 to 1881, came from Ohio—and not even, in the beginning, to attend Harvard. His successor at the *Atlantic*, Thomas Bailey Aldrich, was from New Hampshire. (Aldrich, a familiar figure on Boston Common as he strolled from his home on lower Pinkney Street to his favorite restaurant, Locke-Ober's in Winter Place, described himself in later life as "not genuine Boston, but Boston plated.") Dr. Alexander Graham Bell was born in Scotland, but it was in his laboratory just below the top of Beacon Hill that in 1876 the telephone was born. Frederick Law Olmsted, the landscape architect of New York City's Central Park, settled in Brookline in 1886 and subsequently became the father of the Boston Park System. But perhaps the most controversial, surely the most flamboyant, of the late-nineteenth-century émigrées was Isabella Stewart Gardner of New York who collected art and interesting people, entertained with rare style, often shocked "cold roast" Boston society and eventually built a replica of a Venetian palazzo to receive her treasures, to be opened to the public a year after her death as the Gardner Museum.

In these later Victorian years, Bostonians' long-standing Puritanical prejudice against the theater relaxed. Consequently, by the mid-seventies there were never fewer than twenty legitimate playhouses operating, if not always flourishing, in the city—sporting such imaginative and distinctive names as The Siege of Paris Opera House (not actually an opera house in the modern sense), Hooley's, the Boston Museum, the Aquarial Gardens, the Howard Athenaeum (in its final incarnation, the "Old Howard" of burlesque fame), and offering a varied and, on the whole, cosmopolitan dramatic fare. The famous Joseph Jefferson brought his perennially popular *Rip Van Winkle* to town for a run of several weeks. (He had been playing nothing else for twelve years before reaching Boston!) Helena Modjeska, the celebrated and, as everyone said, "gentle" Pole, and "the divine Sarah" Bern-

7

Howard Athenaeum in 1865—later the fondly remembered "Old Howard" burlesque house.

hardt both played, although at different times, in *Adrienne Lecouvreur*. In May, 1875, the same month in which what was to become Locke-Ober Café came into formal existence, the only Boston woman to achieve international fame on the stage, Charlotte Cushman, finally brought her brilliant career to a close playing Lady Macbeth, the part that had launched her on the road to fame at the Tremont Theater forty years before. (It is also interesting to know that according to *King's Handbook of Boston* [1878], Louis Ober "had a few rooms for transient guests [which] were always occupied by noted or wealthy foreigners, among whom were the members of the Italian and the Aimée Opera Companies.") In November of 1878, another (light) opera company came to town to present what was to be the American premiere of Gilbert and Sullivan's *H. M. S. Pinafore* at the Boston Museum Theater. In the chorus was an obscure seventeen-year-old soprano, Lillian Russell, whose later theatrical triumphs, several marriages, liaison with "Diamond Jim" Brady and miscellaneous high jinks would keep tongues wagging for the next forty years. In 1885 she was in Boston again, this time to star in the now long-forgotten musical *Polly* and by then she had become generally established as "The American Beauty" and the paradigm of the Elegant Eighties. So it was no wonder that in her honor an admirer at Locke-Ober's created a dessert, vanilla ice cream in half a cantaloupe, which has since taken its place on countless menus as—what else?—the Lillian Russell.

Nevertheless, in spite of attractions like these, entertaining in those days was for the most part carried on in private houses and almost invariably centered around the tea or dining table. And since current history then was never recorded by the poor and seldom by the middle class, there are left to us only the observations of those who were fortunate enough

9

Lillian Russell in her favorite profile pose.

to participate in the marathon dining divertissements that were laid on in the great houses or, alternatively, in clubs, hotels, or the private dining rooms at Mr. Ober's Restaurant Parisien. One of those guests has left the menu of a dinner which Mr. Thomas Mack provided for his friends in the late seventies:

10

Chateau Yqem Grand Vin

Little Neck Clams

SOUP

Yriarte Pale

Clear Green Turtle aux Quenelles　　*Potage a la Reine*

FISH

Schloss Johannesberger

Soft Shell Crabs, Sauce Tartar

Pommery and Grand "Sec" Carte Blanche

REMOVES*

Filet of Beef Larded, à la Triano

Green Goose Puree Chestnuts

ENTRÉES

Sweetbreads à la Toulouse　　*Broiled Fresh Mushrooms*

Supreme Spring Chicken aux Truffles

Pâté de fois Gras à la Belveu

Roman Punch

GAME

Château Mouton Rothschild

Upland Plover　　*Doe Birds*

SWEETS

Parisienne Soufflée　　*Opera Biscuit*

Chantilly Cream　　*Petits Charlotte en Casse*

Roquefort and Camembert Cheese　　*Olives*

DESSERT

Hamburg Grapes　　*Apricots*　　*Cherries*

Strawberries　　*French Fruit*

Café Noir　　*Ice Cream Sherbet*　　*Pousse Café*

　*Removes: According to *Larousse Gastronomique*, remove is a "dish which in French service *relieves* (in the sense that one sentry relieves another) the soup or fish. This course precedes those called entrées." *Relève*, to be encountered later, is properly a synonym for *remove* and some American menus used both terms, one preceding entrées and one following.

11

One would like to think, probably erroneously, that some of these dishes were not obligatory but simply available from trays or side tables; still, they must have represented a truly formidable challenge to the human digestive system, although six wines possibly postponed that realization until the morning after. In any event, such repasts represented an increasing degree of sophistication and affluence which, especially as the century wore on, were sometimes carried to ridiculous extremes. No gourmanderie or entertainments at a public place in Boston would ever approach the silliness of a dinner laid on by a C. K. G. Billings at Sherry's Restaurant in New York at which the thirty-six presumably horsey male guests—in white ties, tail coats and riding boots—were actually required to dine while bestride the backs of thirty-six horses provided by a local livery stable, their trays attached to the pommels of the saddles. In Boston, public dining was understandably more staid.

Among the hotels, the original Parker House, built in 1854 (the present building dates from 1921), could always be relied upon for excellent food available in abundance, as this menu for "W. H. H." in 1874 indicates:

Oysters on Shell

SOUP

Terrapin   A la Reine

FISH

Fresh Salmon   Cream Sauce

REMOVES

Capons with Cauliflower

Mongrel Goose   Barbed Turkey

ENTRÉES

Sweetbreads with Fresh Peas

Chicken Croquettes   *Fritters au Sucre*

RELÈVES

Galantine Poularde au Truffle   *Pâté de fois Gras Gelée*

GAME

Canvas Back Ducks   *Larded Quail*

Young Black Ducks

PASTRY

Parisienne Soufflée   *Naples Ice*

Biscuit Glace   *Pistachio Cream Meringues*   *Wine Jellies*

DESSERT

Pears   *Bananas*   *Malaga Grapes*   *Oranges*   *Prunes*

Nuts   *Crystallized Fruits*   *Harlequin Ice Cream*

Bon Bons   *Fancy Cake*   *Fruit Ices*   *Olives*

COFFEE

An interesting feature of Victorian menus is the variety of wild game available for them. During the fall and winter, any market worthy of the name offered goose, canvas back duck, black duck, mallard, teal, quail, plover, woodcock, partridge, grouse and venison. In the menu above, incidentally, the mongrel goose and barbed turkey were males, considered especially tender and succulent.

Across Tremont Street from the Parker House was the renowned Tremont House, built in 1828 and destined to carry on into the nineties. This establishment, with a capacity for two hundred and fifty guests, which appears charmingly in many old prints of Boston, had a reputation for gracious hospitality and its dining room offered a superior cuisine with a

Among Boston hotels in the late nineteenth century, the Parker House was especially esteemed for the richness and variety of its table.

more or less international flavor. One of its other noteworthy features was its battery of mechanical water closets, the first in the city. It was in the Tremont House, incidentally, that Louis Ober managed a barbershop for a number of years and one can only wonder whether propinquity—dining room to barbershop—had anything to do with his decision to become a restaurateur.

The Hotel Vendome, built in the Back Bay and now, alas, converted to apartments, was a palatial example of French Victorian architecture and its dining room, with elaborately carved woodwork, impressive mirrors and heavy carpeting, was the epitome of Victorian elegance. To almost the end of its existence as a hotel, the Vendome cuisine was rated highly by connoisseurs.

Another famous hotel landmark was the Revere House, built in 1847 in Bowdoin Square. It was noted for its general air of comfort and excellent cuisine and attracted such notables as the Prince of Wales, later Edward VII, when he came to Boston in 1860, the Brazilian Emperor Dom Pedro, President Grant, the Grand Duke Alexis of Russia, the Hawaiian King Kalakaua, Jenny Lind and Daniel Webster, who is reputed to have delivered many speeches from its iron-railed porticoed balcony.

Besides the Boston clubs with their own quarters and a variety of attractions other than food, in the latter part of the nineteenth century the institution of the informal dining club became increasingly popular. This could comprise a membership which was essentially literary, political, professional or quite diverse in its individual members' interests, and joining together almost solely for the convenience of a dependable luncheon or dinner headquarters. (The Central Lunch Club, for instance, had a membership of a hundred and twenty-five

The elegant Tremont House in the 1870s, where Louis Ober served a term managing the barber shop.

and was composed largely of bankers, brokers and merchants in the State Street area.) Their merits are described in an article in the *Boston Transcript* of April, 1893. The writer begins rather wistfully by commenting that "the most fortunate man is he who can spare the time to go leisurely home and lunch at his own table, surrounded by his own family, but there are comparatively very few who are able to do this." Then acknowledging that the best substitute for this situation is a good club which, however, demands "a very gentlemanly income," our reporter goes on to say that "next to one's club in point of comfort and convenience is the institution known as the dining club. This is the pleasantest and most advanced form of eating one's lunch downtown. Nearly every hotel downtown is the home of several, and they can be found also at the best restaurants. They are composed of men whose interests or tastes bring them together, they meet in a private dining room set apart for their use, and they encourage strongly a flow of wit and soul, as well as other vintages.

"The merits of the dining club can be fully appreciated only by those who have been or are members of one. Everyone who has been obliged day after day to dine in promiscuous and often displeasing company can imagine what must be the pleasure, in the midst of the business routine of the day, to find oneself among a company of sympathetic friends with whom for a short while the biting cares of the world may be forgotten. The body and brain and heart are refreshed at once, and spirits and inspiration are kept flourishing. These clubs range from such as the Tiffin Club—with several hundred members and magnificent quarters of its own—down to informal associations of a dozen members each." The quality of food prepared at these "utilitarian" clubs must have ranged in quality from one end of the spectrum to the other. But what

The Hotel Vendome in the 1880s, the elegant dowager of Boston's Back Bay.

matter? The camaraderie, "the flow of wit and soul" were the main things.

For those who were unable to lunch at home "surrounded by their families," who, alas, had no club to go to for a meal or were intimidated by hotel dining room prices (in 1885, 50¢ for roast beef, turkey or duck, 40¢ for fresh lobster, 10¢ for mashed potatoes, 15¢ for apple pie), Boston supported several hundred restaurants in the seventies, eighties and nineties. Few were distinguished for either cuisine or atmosphere, to be sure, but they offered a wide variety of foods from which to choose—American, French, German, Italian, Chinese, the list read much as it does now. The Union Oyster House still flourishes today in a onetime house built between 1713 and 1714, in Union Street where it was founded in 1826, featuring seafood as it did then. The popular Durgin-Park, founded by John E. Durgin and E. G. Park, began to serve family-style meals in 1832 and still does so. That is, one is seated at a long table with unidentified diners and is served generous portions of substantial, plain American fare as it might have been delivered up at a family dinner in great-grandmother's time.

A favorite restaurant of college men was Billy Park's at Montgomery Place and Bosworth, which flourished for almost fifty years after its opening in 1845. The menu featured steaks, chops and lobster, and a specialty of the house was a distinctive ale known to the clientele as "old musty," which was served in pewter tankards. According to legend, "old musty's" recipe had been provided by an old lady who once lived on the Duke of Rutland's estate, where it had originally been made. Years after his retirement, Billy Park would recall to a reporter, who no doubt had a flair for putting words in his subject's mouth, that "on the occasion of great athletic events at Harvard, the cheers of the cantab (Cantabrigian!) howlers sounded above all the noises on Bosworth."

Another popular steak and chop house was the Coolidge Café, established in Bowdoin Square in 1883, where diners could watch the cooking of their orders on great coke fires beneath huge hoods. Silver grills prevented the meat from being burned by the flaming fat.

Jake Wirth's has been at the same location on Stuart Street since 1868, specializing in hearty German foods and beer, and is distinguished by its sawdust-covered floors and, like Locke-Ober's, some of the oldest waiters, in terms of continuous service at one restaurant, in the city.

A restaurant which must intrigue the fancy of the modern reader was Whitney's Breakfast and Dining Rooms which occupied the upper floors in the "lofty" Equitable Building at Milk and Devonshire Streets. Moses King in his *Handbook of Boston* was taken with the novelty of "three elevators, running constantly by steam power, which carry up and down about 3000 people per day." Another amenity was a "Harvard Room" fitted up "expressly for Harvard students," whatever that may mean. Anyway, again according to King, "these rooms are at a greater elevation from the street floor than any dining rooms in the world, and the only ones in Boston where a genuine English mutton chop, weighing a full pound before it is cooked, can be obtained."

In the 1880s, a remarkable institution appeared on the Boston scene. It was called Thompson's Spa and its staples were such Yankee standbys as baked beans, fish cakes, frankfurters, brown bread and the like—all served at counters. Our *Transcript* correspondent was quite right when he said, in 1893, that "probably no restaurant in Boston holds a higher place in the affections of the public at large than the Spa" (eventually there were several, all now gone). He goes on to say that "the walls are covered with mirrors and signs of temperance drinks, and there is a soda fountain that will give forth any drink sanctioned by the Prohibition Party. And behind the counters are some of the nicest girls you will find in Boston who preside over pies and cakes and eclairs and sandwiches of every description," he concludes with an air of one speaking from experience.

According to our correspondent, though, the owner of Delmonico's in Pie Alley—no connection with New York's famed Delmonico's—had less wholesome inclinations. "A word of regret and reminiscence might be said for Delmonico's" his story goes. "After flourishing long and happily, he finally fell into the snares of the lovely woman who scrubbed floors for him and one morning the doors of his refectory were closed. He had fled with the scrub lady, leaving nothing behind him but a wife, several small but interesting children and a few memories."

Just outside of Winter Place, where Locke-Ober's was to be, A. C. Ludington had a restaurant on Winter Street which was familiarly known as "old Lud's," and Pierce's Oyster Rooms occupied a building directly across the street at No. 6. The histories and characteristics of both establishments have unfortunately been lost in the mists of time, but we do know that above Pierce's was the gymnasium of Mr. T. Belcher Kay which, according to a contemporary report, was "a popular place of resort for the athletic men of Boston who are here taught the art of self defense. Many of the finest young men in Boston resort to these rooms to perfect themselves in the 'manly art,' with varying results." And, no doubt, to develop appetites which Mr. Pierce and "old Lud" attended to.

*An animal swallows its food; a man eats it,
but only a man of intellect knows how to
dine.*

JEAN ANTHELME BRILLAT-SAVARIN

IN THE Victorian era, while restaurants dotted every
section of Boston—contemporary guidebooks say there were
upwards of five hundred—many were "pubs" or "taverns"
which kept going out of business and being revived under
different names, and many served only the plainest, minimal
meals. Consequently the city did not develop a reputation for
public gastronomy until well into the present century. In
these circumstances, it was natural that Boston cooks and
hostesses, thrown onto their own resources, would attain a
commendably high standard in the preparation and serving
of foods and, moreover, would not be by any means restricted
to native dishes. To be sure, the cuisine in the average Victorian household read almost like a restaurant or hotel dining
room bill of fare. For example, Helen Lyon Adamson, in her
fine book, *Grandmother in the Kitchen*, details what three

22

meals could comprise on a typical weekday (Sundays and holidays naturally demanded greater efforts):

BREAKFAST:

Hominy and Heavy Cream with Maple Sugar
Breakfast Beefsteak with Hashed-in-Cream Potatoes
Buckwheat Cakes, Bacon, Hot Syrup and Melted Butter
Apple Pandowdy with Sweet Sauce
Tea or Coffee

DINNER:

Green Pea Soup with Diced Salt Pork
Boiled Ham with Cake Icing and Egg Sauce
Potato Croquettes and Escalloped Tomatoes
Home-made Bread and Freshly Churned Butter
Coleslaw, Pickles, Sweet 'n' Sour, Catsup
Dan'l Webster Pudding, Boston Cream Pie
Tea or Coffee

SUPPER:

Creamed Chicken Shortcake with Butter Sauce
Cold Sliced Ham and Boiled Ox-tongue
Baked Potatoes and Succotash
Muskmelon Pickles, Chow-Chow, Spiced Peaches
Buttered Tremont Biscuits and Cottage Cheese
Almond-Vanilla Blancmange and Election Cake
Milk or Tea

Even when a dinner or supper did not mark a special occasion, several wines could, and usually did, accompany the various courses—sherry with the soup, sauterne with the fish, a chablis or claret with the meat, port or burgundy with the game, and port, sherry and/or claret with the dessert.

This performance is all the more remarkable when one remembers the equipment and conditions it was necessary to cope with—the generally ill-lighted basement kitchen, the hooded coal range that required continual stoking (sometimes even an open spit in a fireplace), the icebox (overdamp and usually too small), the not always efficient dumbwaiter, the necessity of mixing and blending everything by hand. Also, as difficult as it is to imagine now, there were very few cookbooks available to guide either the neophyte or the more experienced cook who wished to broaden her culinary repertoire. In fact, the first "scientific" cookbook, combining recipes for flavorful meals with sound nutritional principles, didn't appear until 1896 when Fannie Merritt Farmer, "Principal" of the Boston Cooking School, produced *The Boston Cooking-School Cook Book*. Fannie Farmer's no-nonsense approach to the problem of cooking assumed absolutely no prior knowledge or experience on the part of the cook. When she said early on, "Cooking is the art of preparing food for the nourishment of the body," "Water is a transparent, odorless, tasteless, liquid" (obviously never having taken a glass in Valparaiso, Indiana), or "A cooking stove is a large iron box set on legs," one didn't perhaps immediately begin drooling. Still, she did run the gamut from the boiling of water to the compilation of the ingredients of eighty-six sauces, and the early editions of her book, with their hundreds of realistic recipes, are avidly sought after today by practical cooks as well as bibliophiles. One of her menus will illustrate the sophistication of her culinary interests:

24

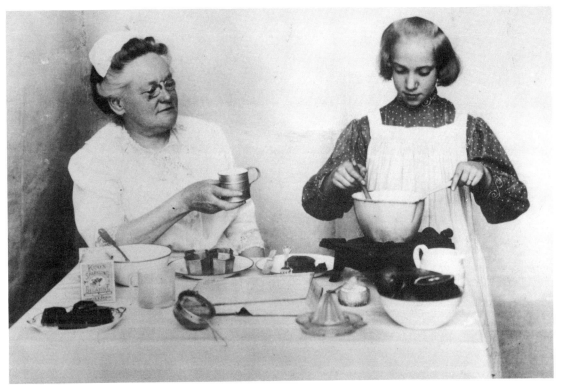

The young girl with Fannie Merritt Farmer deserved a Special Award for Public Service. It was she who suggested that all the ingredients in Miss Farmer's trailblazing cookbook should be given in exact weights and measures.

Little Neck Clams
Consommé au Parmesan
Olives   Salted Pecans
Bouchées
Fillets of Halibut à la Poulette with Mayonnaise
Tomatoes   Delmonico Potatoes   String Beans
Larded Fillet of Beef with Horseradish Sauce
Glazed Sweetbreads
Artichokes with Béchamel Sauce
Sorbet

25

Broiled Quail with Lettuce and Celery Salad
Bananas   Cantaloupes
Sultana Roll with Claret Sauce
Cinnamon Bars   Lady Fingers   Bonbons
Crackers   Cheese
Café Noir

Incidentally, since one of the longtime specialties at Locke-Ober's Café is sultana roll with claret sauce (see page 188), one can't help wondering whether Fannie Farmer perhaps lives on with a special piquant symbolism in Winter Place.

But if the Victorian cook, hostess (and restaurateur, for that matter) labored under certain physical difficulties—which of course probably never occurred to them at the time—there were compensating factors, one of which was the availability of some foods it would be next to impossible to put one's hands on today, at least in this country. Witness a dinner laid down by the Boston Consulate of Haiti at Taft's Hotel at Point Shirley in Winthrop, Massachusetts, in 1880 which, inexplicably to the modern reader, consisted mainly of fish and game, with the accent heavily on the latter:

Steamed Paper Shell Clams
SOUP
Fish Julienne
FISH
Taft's Turbot, King of the Sea
Sea Trout   Weak Fish
Roman Punch (in forms)
GAME
Chicken Grouse   Chicken Partridge
Erie Black Duck

26

Erie Teel
Dough Birds   First of Season
Upland Plover
Chicken Woodcock
Jack Snipe   Grass Birds
Rail   Peeps
Humming Birds, Served in Nut Shells
DESSERTS
Fancy Pastries   Jellies
Fruits in Season
Creams
Stilton   Queen Olives   Water Biscuits
Black Coffee
High Life

Surely it is an exotic and idiosyncratic menu and it requires some comments. Dough birds (sometimes called doe birds) were Eskimo curlews or "owls of the north," and if that year they were the first of the season, they may also have been the last since the species was almost extinct. A jack snipe is technically a European variety of snipe, but the designation may have been used to embellish the menu somewhat. Peeps are small sandpipers and one wonders how in the world they were caught. A rail is a small wading bird related to the crane. Now for the humming birds: the fellow who shot them for Orray Taft of Taft's Hotel confessed that they were actually bank swallows, that is, swallows with nests in holes in the sides of hills.

The Roman Punch on the menu was not a beverage, as might be supposed, but actually an ice comprising fruit juices, wine, rum and meringue, perhaps in this case molded in the shape of a fish and served between courses to freshen the palate.

While the menu of the Haitian Consul's dinner reminds us that our forefathers' appetites were strongly oriented to small game birds, it only begins to indicate the extent of that inclination. More startling are the comments in Moses King's now charming *Handbook of Boston Harbor* (1882) in which the author says that at Mr. Taft's hotel "oftentimes as many as threescore distinct species of game are kept in stock at once, the birds being numbered by the thousands." And he goes on to say that "it is *au règle* for the Boston gentleman to drive, with his visitors from the South or West, over the short and pleasant road to Point Shirley, and there . . . to test the bewildering variety of dainty dishes which Taft has on his menu, from Illinois grouse and Erie ducks to Delaware rail and reedbirds, Jersey willets, a great variety of snipe and plover, and [as we know] humming-birds served in nut-shells."

The table attracts more friends than the mind.

PUBLILIUS SYRUS

PROBABLY LITTLE need be said about the atmosphere in which the affluent Victorian—and Edwardian—was accustomed to dining. On the table, damask cloth and napkins, English china, Waterford or Bohemian or Sandwich glass, coin or heavy plated silver. The woodwork was dark, natural or stained. The walls papered, sometimes with rich embossed designs, and finished with deep molded cornices. The ceilings smooth plastered, but often with a raised medallion in the center above a chandelier. The floors carpeted from wall to wall in colorful figured designs and overlaid here and there with oriental scatter rugs. The lighting, brass chandelier and side lights with electricity or gas and often a combination of the two. On the walls of the dining room, as well as practically every other living space of the house "above stairs," and not excepting the hallways, there was usually displayed a remarkable eclecticism for there tended to be a profusion of pictures

29

of every description—oils, watercolors, steel engravings, family photographs—encompassing a myriad of subjects: family, genre, pastoral, mythological, historical, patriotic and on and on. And everywhere in the Victorian house in town, house in the country, or apartment, the rooms, even the dining room so far as possible, were stuffed with a bewildering collection of seemingly unrelated items—lamps, pillows, china cabinets, coat racks, plaster and marble figures, dried flowers, fans, wicker pieces, stringed musical instruments, footstools, shawls and other knicknacks. William Dean Howells aptly described a typically furnished home of the period in *A Hazard of New Fortunes:*

"Everything had been done by the architect to save space, and everything to waste it by Mrs. Grosvenor Green. She had conformed to a law for the necessity of turning round in each room, and had folding-beds in the chambers; but wherever you might have turned round she had put a gimcrack so that you would knock it over if you did turn. Every shelf and dressing-case and mantel was littered with gimcracks. The front of the upright piano had what March called a short-skirted portière on it, and the top was covered with vases, with dragon candlesticks, and with fans. The floors were covered with filling, and then rugs, and then skins; the easy-chairs all had tidies, Armenian and Turkish and Persian; the lounges and sofas had embroidered cushions hidden under tidies. The radiator was concealed by a screen, and over the top of this some Arab scarfs were flung. There was a super-abundance of clocks. China pugs guarded the hearth. Some red Japanese bird-kites were stuck about in the necks of spelter vases, a crimson umbrella hung open beneath the chandelier, and each globe had a shade of yellow silk."

None of which, however, seemed to affect the contemporary diner's gusto adversely, judging from the menus that have been left us.

The penchant for overfurnishing interiors was also manifest in the restaurants and public dining rooms of the period, and it was a spartan establishment indeed that didn't reach its quota of pictures, mirrors, potted palms, stuffed deer heads, busts on pedestals, chandeliers and assorted examples of the owner's or manager's decorating whims.

*The art of dining well is no slight art, the
pleasure not a slight pleasure.*

MONTAIGNE

Boston is so rich in historical associations that it
would be difficult to stand on almost any corner and not be
within a stone's throw of some notable relic of the past. Winter
Place, where Louis Ober and Frank Locke started their respec-
tive enterprises in the seventies and eighties of the last century, is no exception. A few steps from the Common, the Old
Granary Burying Ground and "Brimstone Corner" (the site
of the Park Street Church), Winter Street, from which Winter
Place debouches for a few yards, was known originally as
Blott's Lane after an early settler, but by 1708 had become
Bannister's Lane. Winter Street and Winter Place were, as
was all the surrounding area, largely residential until the
middle of the nineteenth century. The patriot, Samuel Adams,
had a house on the southeast corner of Winter Street and
Winter Place which he moved to in 1784, since his house on
the waterfront had been too damaged to return to after being

"Brimstone Corner," a stone's throw from Winter Place and virtually the hub of The Hub—in 1900.

requisitioned by the British army. Other residents of Winter Street were T. B. Wales, a rich shipowner; J. F. Priest, a wealthy ironmonger; James Means and George Trott, merchants and neighbors; and William Beals of the *Boston Post*. At the upper entrance to Winter Street lived one of the town's foremost physicians, Dr. John Homans, while on the northern corner stood Mrs. Dexter's boarding house "where lived a number of the best people, among them some gentlemen occupying high public positions." Near the lower end of the block, the handsome Greek-pillared Central Congregational Church was built in 1841, no doubt an added convenience for Mrs. Dexter's guests.

An alternative entrance to Winter Place is through a narrow passageway from Temple Place, which is also not without some historical interest. Until 1864 it was a cul-de-sac, the lower end linked to Washington Street only by a flight of wooden steps. Because of this characteristic, it was long known as Turnagain Alley, until in fact 1830 when a Masonic temple was built on the street which suggested the name Temple Place. It was also the site of one of the most spacious and elegant mansions of the time, that of Colonel Thomas Handasyd Perkins, merchant and philanthropist, whose mammoth portrait by Sully hangs in the Boston Athenaeum.

Winter Place itself, in the middle of the nineteenth century, was "a pleasant residential block of some half a dozen houses, occupied by well-to-do families . . . facing the rear garden of Colonel T. H. Perkins, with its choice shrubbery and fragrant flowers." A little later that garden and many houses and their lots between Tremont Street and Winter Place were swallowed up by Shepard, Norwell & Company, for almost a century one of the city's largest dry-goods stores. Another dry-goods store, Jordan Marsh and Company (as it then styled itself), had taken over a building half a block down from Winter Place in 1861 and a few years later its principal owner, Eben Dyer Jordan, would have something important to contribute to Louis Ober's decision to strike out on his own as a restaurateur.

One works well who dines well.

LOUIS XIV

THE OCCUPANTS of the Winter Place houses just before the advent of Ober and Locke have more or less fugitive identities today. One was Albert Fearing, a merchant, another was Frederick Brown, a druggist, and at about that same time William Lowell owned No. 4.

It was only a short stroll along Tremont Street from the Tremont House, where Louis Ober had the barbershop, to Winter Street and thence to Winter Place, so Ober would have been familiar with the neighborhood and apt to hear about any commercial possibilities becoming available in Winter Place. After all, several private houses on Winter Street had already given way to trade and entertainment. The latter was represented by the historic and majestic Boston Music Hall (currently the Orpheum Theater) at the end of a short cul-de-sac, Music Hall Place, almost directly opposite Winter Place. Here such notables as Ralph Waldo Emerson, Wendell Phillips, William James and Oscar Wilde appeared; Tchaikovsky's Con-

35

In Locke-Ober's early days, the famous Boston Music Hall was almost directly across the street from the entrance to Winter Place. The building it occupied still stands.

certo No. 1 and Saint-Saens' Concerto No. 2 had their world premieres; and the term "Boston Brahmin" is said to have derived from the hardihood of an audience that took a performance of Brahms' then controversial Symphony No. 2 in its stride. As for business, Mrs. Meyer was conducting a confectionery at No. 20, Maturin Ballou was publishing *Ballou's Pictorial* at No. 22, and G. C. Clapp had set up a printing shop at No. 24. More interestingly, in 1868, F. A. Blanc was operating a restaurant at No. 4 Winter Place when Louis Ober, quite possibly one of his patrons, decided to take it over. The shift to the role of restaurateur, however, represented a sharp break from any of the occupations in Ober's past and it can only be speculated why he took this opportunity to strike out in a new direction. Born in the French department of Alsace in 1837, he had been brought to this country by his parents at the age of fourteen. The Obers first settled in the Williamsburg section of Brooklyn, where young Louis went to work grinding watch crystals, but before long they moved to Newark, New Jersey. From that time until he finally drifted to Boston, probably in the early fifties, he practiced a number of trades—barbering, taxidermy, bookselling, picture frame making, produce buying and shipping—in Cincinnati, Philadelphia and New York. And somewhere along the way, in addition to the French and German he had brought with him from Alsace, he developed a fluency in Italian and Spanish. Louis Ober was, then, by the time he came to terms with Mr. Blanc, comparatively a man of the world. He had traveled, he knew languages, he had a civilized European background. He was ready to put his experience and growing sophistication to use in some enterprise of his own. The availability of Mr. Blanc's restaurant offered that opportunity to a man who could see how all over the central part of Boston business blocks were

In the 1870s, "trade"—like the publisher of Ballou's Pictorial—*was beginning to displace the solid residences in Winter Place.*

displacing houses, and these business blocks would contain people, lots of people, all of them with appetites.

The "cellar restaurant" at No. 4 Winter Place survived even the Panic of '73. Businessmen in the area—and Washington Street by now was solidly devoted to trade—found it, if not quite the same thing as taking the midday meal at home, at least a bearable alternative. And from the private houses that remained above Washington Street as well as those across

Washington Street in the 1890s, with Eben Jordan's department store on the right.

the Common on Beacon Hill, the supper patronage steadily grew, attracted no doubt by such dishes as hot leek and potato soup, and beef stew, both of which years later were transmuted into cold Vichyssoise (page 133) and Casserole of Beef Chasseur (page 160), and frequently appear on Locke-Ober's menu today. Ober's French background would perhaps have accounted for another still popular dish at Locke's, Coq au Vin Bourguignonne (page 149), but for the most part he would limit the bill of fare to such standbys as Chicken Pot Pie à la Winter Place (page 152), Thick English Lamb Chop with

39

Kidney (page 176), New England Boiled Dinner (page 159) and Indian Pudding (page 186). Presently Ober's fortunes took an even more favorable turn. One of his most appreciative customers was Eben Jordan, mentioned earlier, head of the thriving Jordan Marsh emporium just down the street. As a boy, Jordan had come to Boston from Maine in 1836 (with $1.25 in his pocket) and greatly prospered. Now, in 1875, when the opportunity presented itself for Ober to acquire the buildings at both No. 3 and No. 4 and expand upwards, Jordan offered his financial support. In precisely what amount is not known, but it must have been crucial for to this day a large round table in one of the broad first-floor windows is reserved for Jordan Marsh executives at noontime, symbolic of a friendly financial bond and a debt that was paid years and years ago.

Because the purchase of Nos. 3 and 4 demanded a substantial outlay of cash, the necessary renovations that followed were just extensive enough to convert the building for a specialized business purpose. Accordingly, the main dining room and kitchen occupied the first floor while space was found for two private dining rooms on the second. The remainder of the second floor and part of the third were reserved for the Ober family's living quarters.

While the remodeling of Nos. 3 and 4 Winter Place was an obvious basic necessity and consequently important in the career of Louis Ober, another innovation profoundly indicated the direction he intended the enterprise to take. He named it Ober's Restaurant Parisien—a pledge and a commitment—and in an illustrated advertising card, he forthrightly claimed to have "the only Restaurant where French Cooking is made a specialty."

Since Ober was essentially an entrepreneur and not himself a cook, the French accent in the kitchen of the new restau-

The only Restaurant where French Cooking is made a specialty   Oyster and Lunch counter for prompt service.   Large Dining-Rooms for ladies and gentlemen. Private rooms for Dinner or Supper Parties.   Open daily till 12 o'clock, P.M.

MR. OBER calls special attention to his large stock of Wines selected by himself, in France. They are recommended by Physicians as pure and wholesome. and are sold Wholesale or Retail at fair prices.

"The only Restaurant where French Cooking is made a specialty"
and, incidentally, where the wines "are recommended by physicians
as pure and wholesome." An advertisement for the early Restaurant
Parisien.

rant must have been obtained either from an authentic French chef, possibly imported specifically for the job, or by a chef with considerable previous experience in the art of French cooking, perhaps in some New York restaurant like Delmonico's. In any event, judging from the manner in which Ober's restaurant developed in subsequent years, the principles laid down at the beginning clearly followed the dicta of the great French chefs and gourmets who flourished in the late eighteenth and early nineteenth centuries—Brillat-Savarin, de la Reyniere, Viard, Louis-Eustach, Beauvilliers and, above all, Antonin Carême (1784–1833), who served Talleyrand, Czar Alexander I, the Prince Regent later George IV, Lord Castlereagh (of Congress of Vienna fame), and the prince of finance, Baron de Rothschild. This "Cook of kings and King of cooks," the undisputed founder of "la grande cuisine," classic French cookery, summed up his life's work and the condition of French cooking in his time in eleven volumes which stressed again and again the importance of shrewd marketing, freshness of ingredients, proper kitchen organization and a systematic culinary nomenclature. And it probably went without saying in the establishment Ober envisaged in 1875 that only the best, the most expensive, ingredients would be used, that quality and service would be as consistent as humanly possible, that every dish would be cooked to order, that the preparation of a dish would never be rushed, and that the same care would be expended on an order of fresh peas as on a fillet of sole, bonne femme. All of these principles, handed down from manager to manager, chef to chef, cook to cook, waiter to waiter, are just as inviolate, just as much in evidence at Locke-Ober's today as they were in 1875.

The "first phase" of Ober's Restaurant Parisien may be said to have covered the years to 1886. At the end of that

The venerable brass check-printing machine, used by the bartenders, became obsolete when the price of drinks exceeded a dollar.

period, *Illustrated Boston: The Metropolis of New England* could say:

"Louis P. Ober, Restaurant Parisienne [sic], Importer of Wines, Nos. 3 and 4 Winter Place.—The city of Boston has long been recognized as the centre where unlimited capital, vast practical experience, and boundless enterprise have combined to make its cafés and restaurants superior to any in this country. As the leading contributor to the reputation of the city in this regard, and as a model establishment of its kind, the Restaurant Parisienne, conducted by Mr. Louis P. Ober, at Nos. 3 and 4 Winter Place, stands pre-eminent. It was opened to the public in 1868 by its present proprietor, a native of sunny France, who came to this city twenty-five years ago, and who brought to bear a thorough knowledge of all the wants and requirements of the business, and quickly acquired a reputation and a patronage that placed his establishment in the foremost ranks of enterprise, popularity and success. Three spacious floors are occupied—the first as an elegant café and lunch-room for gentlemen, the second containing three public lunch-rooms, and the third for private supper-rooms, all arranged and appointed in the most appropriate and recherché style, reflecting the utmost credit upon the good taste and judgment of the proprietor, and insuring the convenience and comfort of all patrons. The cuisine is in charge of chefs of marked ability and national reputation. The management secures its table supplies from the most reputable and varied sources, all the important markets of the country paying tribute to its enterprise. All the delicacies that can possibly be obtained are served in liberal abundance, while the perfect manner in which the viands are served make a meal at Ober's a most agreeable experience. While there are larger restaurants in the country than Ober's, there are none which possess such well-founded claims upon public favor or enjoy a more deserved popularity. Any dish is cooked to order in the best manner, and at moderate prices, while the finest Bordeaux, Burgundy, Champagne, Rhine, and Moselle wines, sherry, port, Madeira, and claret, brandies and liquors, beers and ales, are served of the best quality and imported direct from the most celebrated sources by the proprietor. Attentive and courteous European waiters are in attendance, and the patronage is large, first-class, and influential at all seasons. Mr. Ober is a gentleman of tried ability as a caterer and restaurateur, and is held in universal esteem as an accomplished, reliable,

FOR THE WEEK ENDING SATURDAY, NOVEMBER 15, 1879.

PARK THEATRE PROGRAMME.

OBER'S

Restaurant Parisien

4 WINTER PLACE.

Restaurant a La Carte.

Lunch Counter.

Fancy Oysters.

Private Dining Rooms.

TABLE D'HOTE,

Dinner from 1 to 4 o'clock,   75 Cents.

This place of over twenty years' standing, where French cooking, par excellence, is made a specialty, combining a first-class Restaurant, with Lunch and Oyster Counter for private service; also, Private Dining Rooms for families or parties after concerts or theatrical performances, is respectfully submitted to the patronage of connoisseurs of good cooking.

Wines and Cigars

Of my own importation.

OPEN TILL 12 O'CLOCK, P. M.

L. P. OBER, Proprietor.

An advertisement aimed at theatergoers in 1879.

and representative exponent of this important branch of mercantile activity."

In just eleven years, the business, increasingly profitable, had been accepted as the outstanding French-style restaurant in the region. Its proprietor had been making periodic trips abroad to stock and restock his cellars and at the same time to

45

lure chefs, cooks and waiters to his burgeoning establishment. He was also, while in Europe, observing the operation and decor of restaurants similar to his own, buying paintings and statues (most of which actually went to his palatial estate in suburban Auburndale), and conferring with wood carvers, painters and glaziers—all looking to a grand refurbishing of the Restaurant Parisien which would finally take place in 1886.

I do not think money is ever wasted on a good dinner. If a man dines badly, he forgets to say his prayers going to bed, but if he dines well, he feels like a saint.

SAM WARD

T HE PROCESS of remodeling this time was a great deal more costly and time consuming than the one that had brought the business out of the cellar. First of all, it was necessary to assemble many materials—a quantity of seasoned mahogany from what was then San Domingo, huge plate glass mirrors from France, flocked and etched gold wall coverings, German silver dishes (their massive covers marvelously operated on counterweighted chains), leather upholstered chairs, etched and stained glass, graceful "electrolier" chandeliers, oak wall paneling, and a wonderful hand-operated dumbwaiter of brass on brass poles, which still faithfully lifts drinks from the bar to the dining room above.

Although it would be nice to believe the legend that Ober

The dumbwaiter has been faithfully ferrying drinks from the downstairs bar to the Ober Room since 1886.

brought carvers all the way from France, it is much more likely that he would have found these artisans closer to home —at, for instance, the well-known A. H. Davenport and Company. Davenport, which gave its name to a small still popular writing desk as well as a large upholstered sofa, flourished from 1842 to 1916 and in 1875 had its furniture working shops and showrooms on Washington Street, only a few blocks from Ober's restaurant. For years it supplied expert carvers to Boston architects, builders and decorators (as well as furniture for the White House in Washington), and it would have been the logical place to turn to for this work, now a rare and expensively procured art. Local craftsmen, who today would surely be called artists, were definitely recruited to decorate the ground-floor ceiling.

The intricately carved mahogany is most noticeable on the front of the long L-shaped lunch counter and adjoining bar and around the backbar mirrors and clock, the single large portrait and the vestibule at the front entrance. The workmen who fashioned them didn't presume to sign their work, which is a pity because, as we know now, they practiced an art in the grand tradition. The stained glass in cunning Art Nouveau motifs over the large street-floor windows and in the vestibule strongly resembles that being designed and manufactured by Louis Comfort Tiffany in Brooklyn in the eighties, although similar glass of high quality was being produced by Redding, Baird and Company, just around the corner from Ober's on Franklin Street. The heavy silver steam table covers (still polished weekly, although no longer regularly used) were made by Reed and Barton; they kept food hot on silver platters and in silver tureens and were so ingeniously designed that they can still be lifted by a finger. The finely painted ceiling—rediscovered after washing and restoring in

A detail from the hand-carved mahogany woodwork in the main dining room.

The German silver tureen and platter covers, used only on special occasions, are perhaps the most distinguishing hallmark of the main dining room.

1965—is in essence an Etruscan spring with leaves, lilies, rosettes and mythical animals in soft greens, golds, yellows and rusty pinks, a comprehensive work it would be well nigh impossible to duplicate today.

On the upper floors, the paneled oak wainscoting was surmounted by smooth plastered walls with a raised plaster fleur-de-lis design, still visible in the third-floor hall and in the stairwells. In the second-floor dining room—now known as the Ober Room—heavy booths were constructed with plush seats and rich velvet portieres in the manner of the age, and if no decorous Boston lady could be seen entering one of the strictly private dining rooms farther upstairs except with her husband or family, to be lured into one of these *intime* and upholstered sanctums was probably only a little less daring.

Finally, two pieces of art which escaped transportation to the family home in Auburndale and which still adorn the first-floor dining room were acquired—one purchased by Ober on a European trip and the other commissioned in Boston. The first is a dramatic bronze sculpture about forty-two inches in height called *Gloria Victis*, which stands on a mahogany pedestal in the center of the room and, unfortunately, has been allowed to become an irresistible hat rack. The sculptor, also an accomplished painter, was Marius-Jean-Antonin Mercié, who was born in Toulouse in 1845 and died in Paris in 1916. His career was a long and distinguished one—winner of the Grand Prix de Rome at twenty-three, member of the select French Institute, sometime president of the Society of French Artists and Grand Officer of the Legion of Honor. Interestingly, the original of *Gloria Victis* was his first great success and, in fact, was honored by being installed in the courtyard of the Hôtel de Ville (City Hall) in Paris in 1874. (No visitor to Paris can avoid seeing his figure of Napoleon on its imposing column in the Place Vendôme.) Exactly what *Gloria Victis* represented or symbolized it is now difficult to say but Louis Ober, fervent Alsatian chauvinist that he was, quite possibly saw in it a dream of France rising victoriously again after the military disaster of the 1870 Franco-Prussian War.

The second artwork in the first-floor dining room is probably the best-remembered object in the place, the large nude

Marius-Jean-Antonin Mercié's "Gloria Victis," Boston's most interesting hatrack, in the main dining room.

painting of a young woman always mysteriously referred to as one *Mademoiselle Yvonne*, which stands in its carved mahogany frame on the north wall. Over the years she has endured bad jokes and bad poetry and, whenever Harvard loses a football game to Yale, a black crepe sash, but she is actually the creation of a first-rate painter of the time, Tomaso Juglaris. Juglaris was born in Moncalieri in the Italian Piedmont in 1845. He studied at the Turin Academy of Fine Art and was later a pupil of Thomas Couture in Paris. He exhibited successfully in Turin, at the Beaux Artes in Milan and at the Paris Salon, and in 1879 became Artistic Director of L. Prang and Company in Boston whose famous proprietor, Louis Prang, covered the walls of America in the late eighteenth and early nineteenth centuries with his popular chromolithographs ("chromos") on every conceivable subject. In 1890, he became a professor at the New England Conservatory, the faculty of which included several artists whose works are greatly prized by museums and collectors today. Legend has it that Ober paid $80.00 for the Juglaris painting, which would seem a perfectly reasonable figure for such a work in 1875, but considering the artist's standing in the community at the time, it seems likely that if it was painted in a garret in Bromfield Street, as the story also goes, it was not an unheated one.

There is an interesting postscript to the story of *Mademoiselle Yvonne* which illustrates how our attitudes toward female toplessness have changed in recent years. In 1948, when the restaurant's manager was considering the printing of a postal card featuring the lady to pass out to guests, it was thought necessary to consult the post office "as to the mailability of cards bearing the picture of a nude." The postmaster, however, declined to give an opinion "in advance of its actual deposit in the mails addressed for delivery to addressees" and commented further that "if one harbors doubt as to the mail-ability of material offered, because of the statutes relating to obscenity, a sense of decency and good morals should compel him to conclude that the material should not be sent through the mails." As simple as that. Anyway, upon receipt of this exhortation, it was decided to risk sending Mademoiselle's likeness wherever the writ of the post office department runneth and of course no repercussions have ever been recorded, at least legally.

Louis Ober had finally achieved an ambiance to complement his uncompromising French cuisine. This was the time in which Bacon's *Dictionary of Boston* would warn that the Restaurant Parisien was "most patronized by the possessors of long purses" while happily conceding that "the viands here are unsurpassed by any place in the city." It was the period in which many of the present day specialties of Locke-Ober's were featured. For example, Sweetbreads Eugénie (page 172), in which the thymus glands of young calves were cunningly combined with ham, mushrooms, sherry and a cream sauce and served under a glass bell; Coq au Vin (page 149), a quartered chicken with mushrooms, onions, celery, cherries and Burgundy, cooked in a crock; Filet Mignon, Mirabeau, that hearty perennial favorite of men which must have been prepared originally in the classical manner but has somehow since lost its anchovies and olives in Locke-Ober's recipe (page 156).

To complement his expanding and improving menu, Ober in this period was zealously endeavoring to keep the quality of his wines equally high and doing so at a time when nature seemed intent upon frustrating his efforts. What might

The main dining room on the street floor is little changed from the original Restaurant Parisien of 1876.

be called the golden age of vintage wine had reached its peak in the late seventies when the dreaded phylloxera, an insect that attacked and destroyed the roots of the vines, began devastating the vineyards of Europe, and by 1884 the last of the traditional classic vintages disappeared. After that, grafting from hardier phylloxera-resisting stock began, but recovery was naturally slow and it was not, in fact, until the turn of the century that great vintages appeared on the European scene in any satisfying quantities. Meanwhile, it was necessary to pay higher and higher prices for wines which were not likely to be replaced in the foreseeable future and, alas, these included even the Traminers, Rieslings and Pinots of Alsace to which Ober had always been understandably partial. Through these wine drought years, the flow of beers, ales and "hard" liquors of course continued unabated and there are those who insist that Louis Ober ought to be memorialized for "inventing" the martini with an olive in it, but all that could hardly have compensated financially or emotionally for the long assault on the vineyards of Europe from the seventies onward.

Still, the "second phase" of Ober's Restaurant Parisien was a brief one. In May, 1894, twenty-five years after taking over the old "cellar restaurant" at No. 4, Louis Ober abruptly sold the business to Wood and Pollard, a firm of wholesale liquor dealers. His reasons for doing so are not entirely clear, since the restaurant continued to justify amply the heavy remodeling expenses of a few years before. But two things probably influenced Ober's decision to leave the business. Over the years he had been able to accumulate a considerable estate consisting of securities and city and suburban properties and these investments were demanding more and more of his time and attention. (His obituary in the *Boston Globe*, in July, 1900, mentions that "about fifteen months ago, he had made over $200,000.00 in one deal"—a respectable sum in those days.) Also, in 1892 an energetic competitor had moved into Nos. 1 and 2 Winter Place in the person of one Frank Locke.

*And Noah he often said to his wife when
he sat down to dine,
'I don't care where the water goes if it
doesn't get into the wine.'*

G. K. CHESTERTON

L OCKE WAS BORN in Loudon, New Hampshire, in
March 1848. In 1863, at the age of fifteen, pretending to be
eighteen, he enlisted in the Union Army, going south with
the Second New Hampshire Heavy Artillery. Coming to Boston after the war, he established a saloon which much later
on he described simply as "a thriving business on the corner
of Broad and State Streets." In any case, in due time a professional acquaintance, Dudley S. McDonald, who operated
a confectionery at 16 Winter Street and a restaurant around
the corner on Tremont, agreed to help set him up in a café
on the site of Nos. 1 and 2 Winter Place which McDonald
owned and which had recently been vacated by the Winter
Place Club. Frank Locke's Wine Rooms opened for business
there in 1892.

Frank Locke—unintentional abettor. In time his ambitions
contributed to the total enterprise.

In an elaborate booklet describing the new quarters, Mr. Locke or his publicity genius, after placing the Wine Rooms geographically for the reader, goes on to paint a picture of the interior which is so vivid, detailed and rich in Victorian prose that it must positively be quoted in full to achieve its full effect:

"One passes quite a distance up this Place before the first doorway, or 'No. 1,' is reached. An iron crane projecting into the thoroughfare a few feet from over this doorway holds suspended a gigantic padlock, which upon close examination shows fine proportions and excellent workmanship, and which bears across the top of its exaggerated face the name, 'FRANK,' in gilded letters of most ornate design, the whole device being intended to convey to the beholder the information that the building to which it is attached is the business headquarters of Mr. Frank Locke, a gentleman well known in Boston enterprise for the past three decades.

"The old premises at No. 1 Winter Place were early in the year 1892 completely stripped of the buildings that had occupied them, and in their place there has been erected the present neat and substantial structure that now fills the site, and which is to be the subject of somewhat minute description in this sketch. This new building has been erected especially for the uses of Mr. Locke, who, having been largely successful in his downtown business, was desirous of planting an establishment upon a more pretentious scale, in a quarter of the city eligible for another class of patronage, and in accordance with designs and plans of his own.

"The building is now entirely finished, and the establishment open to public inspection and patronage. The business connected is that of supplying the public with fine wines, liquors and buffet luncheon.

The original Frank Locke's Wine Rooms, 1892.

"The entire front of the building upon Winter Place is taken up by the front door before referred to and a broad show window, admirably glazed and finished. The appearance of this window as seen by the passer-by is of itself a most attractive invitation to enter the place. A bank of mosses, rich and varied in their coloring and suggestive of a cool and tasteful retreat, backs the window for its entire width inside. Over these mosses diminutive palms and green-waving exotic plants are shading; and among and above these on every side rich specimens of artistic production reveal themselves. Provision for the electric lighting is most elaborate in design and finish; and the merest tyro can perceive that the materials employed are costly and the expense in production unstinted.

"A glance within doors, or into the hallway that lies just within the entrance, shows that the window is not a special feature upon which all the resources of the establishment have been lavished; but that it is only a suggestion, as it were, of still further artistic provision within the walls—a frontispiece, so to speak, of a work abounding in delights and beauties.

"Passing through the front doorway, and entering upon the first floor through the hallway or vestibule, which is really a part of it, the visitor is surprised at the vision that immediately opens before him. A step or two inside, and the general appearance is as of an enchanting picture, a fairy grotto, a sumptuous apartment in some palatial edifice. The estimate of the scene varies according as one more or less quickly looks about him. There are beautiful pictures of assured artistic merit upon the walls.

"The flash and glint and glow of mirrors of heavy plate and rich cut glass in myriad forms are on every side. Furniture and fixtures and railings of polished mahogany vie with the mirrors in reflecting all objects within the view. Hangings of costly plush and damask, and walls and arched ceilings covered with embossed and quilted satins, enhance the attractions. A series, not of pictures, but of real cascades, ends in a broad waterfall upon one side, their murmuring and rippling making a music entirely in keeping with that upon which the eye feasts. In various parts electric lights of many colors irradiate bouquets of flowers, artificially and most artistically produced, and furnish an element for shading and coloring in infinite variety at many points, the effects alternating and succeeding each other mechanically or at the will of the proprietor or employees of the establishment.

"All this and much more the eye of the visitor takes in through a few glances about, although at first in a confused and astonished way that requires a little examination of details before the perceptions are clearly satisfied and the scheme of the whole presentation understood.

"This first floor of the establishment is used for the bar and lunch-room, and contains also the business office of the proprietor, with provision for the comfort and entertainment of guests and patrons that will hereinafter be fully described. Assured that the stock in trade provided for patrons and visitors is unsurpassed in quality and variety by any establishment of the kind in the city, some attention may now be given to the details in the construction and furnishing of the place.

"The bar, which occupies a large portion of one side of the room, is of highly finished and polished solid mahogany, plainly and substantially constructed so far as its woodwork is concerned. Its posts and their capitals are of cut glass wrought in elegant patterns and equally substantial and appropriate with the woodwork. It may here be mentioned that cut glass as a material is used lavishly in every part of this room, forming not only an ornamental but a constructive element in its appointments and furnishings.

"The bar rail, extending along the top edge of the whole front of the bar, and at a height convenient for a leaning position of the customer, is a heavy tube of cut and embossed glass clear as crystal, the hollow of which, from end to end, is filled with artificial roses and other beautifully constructed flowers.

"By a device of electric lighting these flowers are made to flash with their natural colors at short intervals; so that while the visitor leans upon the rail, or stands near it in conversation with a friend or those about him, the leaves and petals of these flowers attract wondrously by their occasional illumined revelation, and fascinate him by the originality of their design and novelty of their manifestations. This bar rail is a distinctive feature of this establishment; and in the short time that has elapsed since the place was first opened has attracted largely the attention of persons of artistic tastes, and of others interested in similar establishments in various cities. The supports for this rail, and for very much of the glass work in various portions of this room, are of the finest brass, moulded and wrought into numberless artistic forms. The floor of this room is beautifully tiled, fine effects being produced by introducing at various points imitation rugs and mats, the material of the finest mosaic work known in these departments, with ornate figures and designs as effectively wrought out as though the whole were fine imitations of the most elaborate figures of a carpet factory. This tiling is of itself a most marked feature of the finish of the room.

"Whenever in this room one glances upwards toward the ceiling, the attraction is irresistible to study the effects

66

there found. The construction in this particular is of the ancient type, great beams placed at frequent intervals furnishing the foundation of the flooring of the second story, and apparently depending downward with the proportions almost of bridge timbers. The lower faces of these beams are completely covered with mirror plate, with gilded frame work at the edges running the entire length of the beams. From the lower edges of these beams arches are sprung, there being eleven measuring each about three feet across the base line. They are lined with satin finely quilted in squares, the coloring just a little off white—'firmament blue,' the proprietor styles it.

"These glossy satin linings and the clear glass of the mirrors alternating, the latter reflecting everything animate or immovable below, afford most unique results, and present ever-changing features for observation. The faces of the beams are broad, so that the mirrors have really a most substantial surface; and the combination is remarkably pleasing.

"On the side of the room opposite the bar, and occupying an alcove not quite so long as that fixture, is the lunch-counter, a duplicate of the bar so far as its woodwork is concerned, but without the novel rail and ornaments. This counter fills the space in the front part of the alcove, and is flush with the projections at either end, so that it appears like a half wall set midway in the partition. Behind it a row of lockers and closets occupy the space next the floor, and for two or two and a half feet above it.

"Above these lockers, and filling the whole remaining space of the rear wall of the alcove, is the chief sensational feature of the ornamentation of the room. This is a representation in miniature, vivid and natural in its general design and ensemble, of a section of mountain side. Rock ledges, depressions and declivities, fissures and winding pathways, and the general features of such scenery where natural formations are wild and rugged, are all here produced, with really artistic fidelity and truthfulness. Away up on the mountain a little stream of real water issues from a glen, and, tumbling over rocks, it finally plunges over a ledge in the very center of the scene, its waters dashing and breaking as they reach the bottom, with a naturalness that forms a most fascinating element in the production.

"Below this fall, the water rushes past an old mill, the low, sloping roof and weather-beaten sides of which enhance the picturesqueness of the scene. The mill wheel is slowly churning the water—not a painted wheel, but one which revolves with all the realism of those of our ancestors. At night dim rays of light shine through the dusty windows of the old structure, indicating the industry of the miller and heightening the effect.

"Careful study on the part of the proprietor in the makeup of this miniature scene has resulted in fine light effects by aid of the electric current. As this current is manipulated from the office or behind the bar, the scenery is presented under early morning light, the full blaze of noonday, or tinged with the fading rays of the setting sun, at the manipulator. These effects have not merely the semblance of the natural features they represent—they have very largely the attributes of these elements, at least so far as appearance and faithfulness in coloring, shading and natural light effects are presented for appreciation. The morning light is indeed a soft, fine-toned vraisemblance of the delicate illumination of the morning twilight; while the tinting and stronger light painting of the setting sun's rays are equally natural and truthful in appearance.

"But this is not all that has been attained here in this department. By careful study and arrangement, the mirrors, great and small, on the opposite side of the room, or behind and above the bar, are made to repeat under varying conditions these light effects, so that these manifestations of sunrise, sunset, etc., may be viewed through vistas apparently miles away, or in perspective, which continues their illusions until the light on the mountain top is seen five, ten, even twenty-five miles across apparent intervening space. As these changes and illusions are constantly recurring as one moves about the room, the result is that with every new standpoint a new or modified scene presents itself, and the variety of combinations is practically unlimited.

"The rear end of the apartment is occupied by two side rooms or booths, not entirely secluded or patitioned off from the main room, but sufficiently isolated by screens and hangings for all purposes of privacy or retirement. The screens or railing work which enclose these booths on the room side are again of brass and glass, curiously wrought in most artistic forms and ornaments that are disposed most effectively in their design and construction. Where these railings are most open, and at the entrances and passage-ways of the booths, heavy velvet plush portieres and hangings and curtains of richest damask are provided, their colors and materials blending finely with those of the screens and the surroundings.

"Springing upward from the center of the screens a curiously cut and formed glass receptacle encloses a bouquet of flowers such as are referred to as ornamenting the interior of the bar rail; and these flowers are colored and lighted electrically, as described in the foregoing pages. (Another of these artificial bouquets of flowers similarly contained is found in the front window, high up in the open space.)

"Across the end of the room, or at the back of the booths, a finely-tinted marble shelf or ledge stands, some four or five feet above the floor, and convenient for many purposes as well as highly ornamental. The walls of the booths are covered to the ceiling with richly figured satin, just a shade off the white and corresponding with that of the ceiling—soft to the touch and to the eye. The furniture of the booths is of solid mahogany, rich and plain and without ornamentation.

"The third and only other booth in this apartment is at the front, and occupies the space between the end of the bar and the show window. Its screens and general construction are similar to those just described in the foregoing, and it forms the business office of the proprietor of the establishment. The curiously wrought brass work of the screen and its ornate dependencies of cut glass, repeat at this end of the apartment the effects which are more fully found at the other.

"Some idea of the quality and profusion of the fine glass work in this establishment may be had when it is known that to finish and furnish this apartment has cost Mr. Locke $36,000, a very large portion of which sum was applied to payment for the glass work alone.

"At various points within this apartment fine specimens of art work are to be seen. A beautifully-executed tapestry painting of 'Mary at the Well' hangs upon the wall immediately within the front entrance. The center of each of the three screens that form the partitions for the booths is occupied by a bronze figure, finely wrought and appropriately placed. These figures are the 'Morning Star,' 'Manhood' and 'Phoebus.'

"Behind the bar, and constructed of the same massive mahogany which forms the material of all the woodwork here, are the wine cooler and the cigar cabinet, elaborately finished, and their contents revealed by glass fronts. An extension of the bar at the front end of the room and adjoining the office affords space for a wonderfully designed cigar showcase. This case is made entirely of fine glass plates a half inch in thickness, curiously dove-tailed and clamped together, and with a sliding door of glass on the back side. Both the seller and the buyer have the most complete view of the inside of this case when its contents are in question, and its singular adaptability to its uses is plainly apparent to the visitor at first glance.

"In the provision of appliances for the comfort and satisfaction of patrons of this establishment, the matter of ventilation was not forgotten. At various points in this apartment stand-pipes of brass, each with a bell-shaped mouth or orifice, are found opening into the rooms about half way between the floor and ceiling. Through these pipes currents of air, cooled artificially by contrivances fixed in the basement of the building, are made to pass at the will of the proprietor or overseer. The air for these pipes is taken from a point fifty feet above the roof tree outside, forced with tremendous energy to the basement, whence, after passing over ice surfaces, it is forced into the rooms above. By these means purest, sweetest air is always afforded throughout the building, which is also delightfully cool whenever coolness is required.

"At night-time the interior of this apartment presents a most beautiful appearance. It is illuminated by one hundred and seventeen electric lights, every nook and corner and cranny sharing in the general lighting up, and the arches overhead, with the recesses wherever found, being fairly resplendent in their revelation. The electric plant is in the basement of the establishment, along with the wine storeroom, the toilet rooms, the steam engine and apparatus, and all the accessories and appliances which such a place must call for. The engine which runs the dynamo also provides power for forcing the air in the ventilators, running the ice-cream machines, pumps, etc. The closets are elaborately furnished in marble, having the best sanitary arrangements known to scientific plumbing, and are kept cool and well aired by means of the ventilators mentioned.

"In short, the establishment has been designed to combine every element which would tend to make it inviting—richness, artistic effects, perfect sanitary conditions and comfort; and it is supplied with the finest products of the vine and still, while the culinary department is of the highest order.

"The novel effects which are shown in such lavishness throughout the place, and which have been secured by an unstinted exercise of ingenuity and outlay of money, daily attract large numbers of lovers of art; and to all such a cordial invitation to inspect the establishment is extended. That the gentler sex may not be deprived of the pleasure of viewing these treasures the hours from nine to eleven o'clock in the morning have been set apart for their convenience, and during that time the beauties of the rooms will be shown to them by courteous attendants."

Alas, a mere replica of the gigantic padlock, now inscribed with the words "Locke-Ober," is all that remains of this Victorian extravaganza for the Wine Rooms were closed and abandoned and their artifacts consigned to the junkyard at the beginning of the Prohibition era.

One infers from Frank Locke's own description of his enterprise that what he had set up was, to put it plainly, a saloon with that then familiar Victorian amenity, a "free lunch" counter—a grander, gaudier saloon than most, to be sure, but a saloon all the same. As such, it catered of course to men exclusively, the "gentle sex" welcome only from nine to eleven A.M. and then only to view the wonders of the place. Unfortunately, Locke had but a short time to enjoy the myriad pleasures of the Wine Rooms for he died in April, 1894, at the age of forty-six. Louis Ober was not among the twelve pall-bearers at the high Masonic funeral conducted by the Ancient Arabic Order of the Nobles of the Mystic Shrine—Noble Locke being one of the founders of Boston's Aleppo Temple.

At the same time that Wood and Pollard, wholesale liquor merchants, bought out Louis Ober, mentioned earlier, they also picked up Frank Locke's Wine Rooms from his estate a month after his early death. There could have been two logical financial reasons for adding the Wine Rooms to the Ober package. The purchase could have been a maneuver to prevent two profitable liquor outlets from falling into the hands of a competitor until a friendly buyer could be found to take them over permanently. And if Mr. Locke had run up a sizable account with Wood and Pollard, that might have been liquidated most expeditiously by acquiring all the assets of his business. In any case, it seems most unlikely that Wood and Pollard intended to operate both establishments indefinitely. They did, however, immediately combine the two, and to celebrate the event, so the story goes, the wall separating Locke's from Ober's was broken through and appropriate ceremonies of jubilation conducted, with all the drinks no doubt on the house. At this point, Emil Camus, unquestionably the guiding spirit of the modern Locke-Ober's, enters the picture.

Although Camus flourished as the guiding genius of the restaurant in Winter Place for upwards of forty years (1894–1896 and 1901–1939), he is an elusive biographical subject. There are good reasons for this. He did not arrive on the

73

Emil Camus—managing genius. For forty years he preserved the standards.

American scene, from Paris, until 1890, when he was already in his late twenties. And from all accounts he was a notably taciturn fellow. (He had a particular horror of telephones, perhaps because he felt phone conversations might encourage him to let too many words slip out.) So all we know about Camus' career before Wood and Pollard brought him in to direct the business is that he worked for a time in New York for Louis Sherry, the famous confectioner and restaurateur, then came to Boston where he was employed in the dining room of the old American House, one of the leading local hotels of the day. According to legend, Camus was quiet, reserved—some thought even haughty—and something of a martinet, and it was probably his lifelong insistence on perfection in his staff which in time made him the restaurateur's restaurateur. The portrait of him on the restaurant's second floor could not be more in contrast to those of his predecessors mounted nearby—those two seemingly casual, hearty, outgoing citizens, Locke and Ober, next to the trim, Gallic figure with its neat chasseur's moustache and its tight, buttoned-up costume.

After a two-year baptism at Locke-Ober's, Camus followed his star to California, returning to put together the Locke-Ober Company in 1901 following the bankruptcy of John Merrow, who had headed an organization that operated the Revere House and in 1898 had branched out with the purchase of Locke-Ober's. Merrow's tenure, while it ended bleakly, was not without its lighter moments. There was, for instance, the impromptu invention of the famous Ward Eight cocktail—a whiskey sour with grenadine. The event that inspired the Ward Eight was a gathering at the Ober bar of several members of the Hendricks Club the night before the elections of 1898. The Hendricks Club, unaccountably named after Cleveland's Vice-President, Thomas A. Hendricks, was a Boston west end political operation presided over by Martin Lomasney, otherwise known as The Mahatma, and the caricature of a nineteenth-century Boston Irish politician. (His credo: "The great mass of people are interested in only three things—food, clothing and shelter.") Lomasney, for propriety's sake, only ran every other term for a seat in the General Court (state legislature), a race he invariably won. And since '98 was his "in" year, The Mahatma's supporters at the bar that night called for the on-the-spot creation of a drink to toast his inevitable victory the following day. The Ward Eight was the result—an instant success and a favorite of Locke-Ober patrons ever since. The postscript to the story is slightly ironic: Martin Lomasney was a dedicated teetotaler.

The discovery of a new dish does more for the happiness of mankind than the discovery of a new star.

JEAN ANTHELME BRILLAT-SAVARIN

O N MAY 1, 1901, Emil Camus, under the letterhead of the new Locke-Ober Company (successor to what Merrow had styled The Winter Place Hotel), sent the following letter to the restaurant's known patrons:

LOCKE-OBER COMPANY

BOSTON

Boston, May 1st 1901.

Dear Sir:

We take pleasure in informing you that we have purchased the interests in THE WINTER PLACE HOTEL formerly controlled by Frank Locke and L. P. Ober, and hope you will favor us with your esteemed patronage as in the past.

77

We have secured the services of Mr. J. B. Bailhé, the famous French Chef for many years with Mr. Ober, and his return will be a guarantee of the excellence of our cuisine.

We remain, Dear Sir,
    Very respectfully yours,
        EMIL CAMUS, *Manager*
        Formerly with Louis Sherry, New York.

The nineties had been an unsettled period for Locke-Ober's. Now it was the task of Emil Camus, at the beginning of the new century, to consolidate, to introduce some permanent order into the management of the restaurant and to stamp it with a character which would insure its survival for years to come. The first order of business was of course to organize the kitchen and establish a bill of fare which would combine the most popular and available American and regional dishes with French accents and cooking methods. Thus Camus and M. Bailhé were inspired to use the fish and shellfish from New England waters in offerings like Lobster Savannah (page 136), Baked Clams Casino (page 125), Finnan Haddie Delmonico (page 143), Steamed Finnan Haddie (page 144), and Planked Fillet of Cod, Winter Place (page 142), and prepare them in a manner which would be appreciated by the most cosmopolitan diners. These goals were relatively modest. Camus had no wish to operate an establishment catering to the masses. He was satisfied with a select group of patrons who returned again and again, behaved with decorum, paid their bills and enjoyed the food, drink and hospitality of what he hoped would long be Boston's finest restaurant.

The odds on his doing just that were excellent for he had

taken the reins at Locke-Ober's for the second time in unusually favorable circumstances. Business conditions were generally on the upswing, and the country and region were in a euphoric mood. In fact, early in 1900, the *Boston Herald* editorialized that "if one could not make money the past year, his case is hopeless." In that first year of the new century, the population was to increase by nearly half a million through immigration alone; the country had just emerged from "that splendid little war" with Spain with new territories in faraway places and a decidedly bullish attitude about its importance in the world; in increasing, some thought alarming, numbers young people were leaving the farms and flocking into cities like Boston to seek—and often to find—their fortunes; although wages and salaries were rising, taxes were inconsiderable and the cost of living by present standards almost unimaginable (eggs were 12¢ a dozen and a sirloin steak could be had for 24¢ a pound at the butcher shop); more and more people were feeling it within their means to patronize the theater and sporting events, to travel for pleasure, to ornament their houses, even to acquire the newfangled automobile (there were already eight thousand in some kind of service in 1900), and to entertain and frequent first-class hotels and restaurants. In his charming memoir, *One Boy's Boston*, Samuel Eliot Morison recalled, of this period, that "the Morisons [his mother and father] frequently dined out, either at friends' houses or at restaurants, such as Marliave's and Locke-Ober's." Proof indeed that Camus had lost no time in combining the ingredients which Boston's more affluent citizens appreciated.

Part of Camus' genius lay in his faculty for assembling a seasoned and conscientious staff, all the more important since his temperament inclined him to function more or less behind

79

the scenes, and some of these assistants not only kept things running smoothly but at the same time added a good deal of color to the establishment. Nick Stuhl, Camus' head waiter, was one of these. An Alsatian like Ober before him, he was a bear of a man who padded around the restaurant for some forty years in ancient carpet slippers, trading repartee with the guests, consuming his share of ardent spirits, conjuring up all manner of get-rich-quick schemes which invariably came to nothing.

Stuhl later succeeded Emil Camus as manager—host would probably better describe his function—and after living for many years in quarters on the top floor, he died in 1943 at the age of eighty-two. Much respected by his peers, the professional purveyors of food and drink, he also prized his honorary membership in an elusive organization called the Michael Mullins Chowder and Marching Society. The M.M.C.M.S. was founded—conceived might be a more apt term—in the twenties and was composed largely of staff members of the *Crimson* and the *Lampoon*, Harvard's news and humor publications respectively, whose dinners at Locke-Ober's were not entirely formal. The inimitable (as he later became) Lucius Beebe was one of its charter members and we're indebted to him for reporting that Frederick Vanderbilt Field, a fellow marcher and chowderer, once supplied the crowning ambiance for a convivial dinner on a cold winter evening in the (then) men's dining room, when he hired an "urchin" to stand outside, press his nose against the large plate glass window and look hungry.

Another memorable employee was Charlie Koechling who, after the luncheon hour was over, would put on his derby hat and make the rounds of credit customers whose bills were in arrears. Eventually Koechling succeeded Stuhl

Caruso as the Duke in Rigoletto. *To have served
him sweetbreads was compensation enough.*

as headwaiter, which presumably cut into the time formerly
devoted to informal bill collecting. Beginning in 1894 the
famous oyster bar was the exclusive domain of Charlie King
who practiced his art there until 1944. And Edward Ivaldi
became notable not only for his forty-year association with the
business but also for the fact that he eventually lived to be
over a hundred. As the saying goes, Locke-Ober's must have

been doing something right in those days.

For Boston, as for the country at large, the years from 1900 all the way up to World War I, or what was once called The Great War, were not unlike a long, pleasant summer afternoon, and the mood and atmosphere at Locke-Ober's reflected it. Enrico Caruso, who early in the century thrilled Bostonians with his roles as the duke in *Rigoletto* and as Canio in *I Pagliacci*, never failed to visit Locke-Ober's at least once during a tour. His favorite dish is said to have been Sweetbreads Eugénie (page 172), and though he always dined with his characteristic gusto, incredibly he never left a tip. (The puzzlement ended in the spring of 1918 when, furious with the local music critics' responses to his performances with the visiting Metropolitan Opera, he vowed never to sing in Boston again.) Henry Cabot Lodge, the author of biographies of Hamilton, Webster and Washington but far better known later as a Congressman and United States Senator, continued the steady patronage he had begun as a student at Harvard. Another regular was a fabulous character in his day, Thomas William Lawson. Lawson wrote several books on financial subjects (*Frenzied Finance, Friday the Thirteenth, The Remedy*) but his real métier was freewheeling market speculation, especially in connection with the promotion of the Amalgamated Copper Company, which made him a fortune. John F. "Honey Fitz" Fitzgerald, John Kennedy's colorful grandfather, who had become mayor of Boston in 1905, undoubtedly rubbed elbows with James Michael Curley at Locke's men's bar but they must never have dined there together because the two were bitter rivals in the Democratic party, a rivalry which finally came to a head with Curley's election as mayor in 1912 (the beginning of a long and checkered public career) and Fitzgerald's retirement to private life. The list of

An engaging 1909 menu card "In honor of Mr. George E. McQuesten on his departure for Europe, tendered by a few of his friends." The drawing on the cover may indicate that McQuesten was not to be unaccompanied.

"celebrity" patrons of those days would make a long and miscellaneous one—actors and actresses, artists and musicians, writers, politicians, what were then called "captains of industry," professional men—all were attracted and held by the uniform excellence of the food and the ambiance surrounding its serving.

Although the time was past when formal dining ran on for sixteen or eighteen courses, the habit was only winding down as is indicated by the following dinner given at Locke-Ober's in May, 1909, "in honor of Mr. George E. McQuesten on his departure for Europe" which was "tendered by a few of his friends."

Canape of Fresh Caviar

Little Neck Clams Cocktail

Olives   Radishes   Salted Almonds

Bisque of Lobster*

Terrapin Maryland Style

Braised Hot House Chicken

Artichokes Sautés   Fresh Mushrooms

Parisienne Potatoes†

Roast Spring Lamb

Cold Asparagus, French Dressing

Fresh Strawberry Ice Cream

Fancy Cakes

Cheese Croquettes

Cafe

Moet & Chandon White Seal

Sun Ray Water

* Page 130.
† Page 184.

The joys of the table belong equally to all ages, conditions, countries, and times; they mix with all other pleasures, and remain the last to console us for their loss.

JEAN ANTHELME BRILLAT-SAVARIN

AMERICA'S ENTRY into the First World War raised some problems for dining rooms like Locke-Ober's when various shortages of customary necessities quickly developed— most noticeably in sugar, wheat, meat and coal. With East Indian sugar practically unobtainable due to a lack of ship carriers and European beet sugar crops cut off, the resources of Cuba fell far short of the worldwide demand. And of course sugar substitutes were not yet perfected. Because the country undertook to ship millions of tons of wheat to its new allies, that shortage became an even greater problem which the government, through its Food Administrator, Herbert Hoover, attempted to solve by prescribing a so-called victory bread consisting of only 50 percent wheat flour supplemented by any other cereal the baker had on hand, say, cornmeal or oat or rye flour (the end product usually regrettable). In addition, restaurants were required to observe one completely wheatless meal each day, meaning not only no bread or rolls but no crackers, macaroni, pastries, pies or cakes. Similarly, Tuesdays and Saturdays were declared porkless days and Mondays and Wednesdays merely meatless (presumably Fridays were already semimeatless)—which, because of its fish and shellfish tradition, did not weigh as heavily on Locke-Ober's as it did, say, on a western steak house. Nevertheless the regulations represented one more challenge to the chef's imagination.

The coal shortage, exacerbated by the unusually cold and snowy winter of 1917–18, kept temperatures down in the dining rooms and fires low in the kitchen ranges. In fact, that winter was so severe that at the Boston Navy Yard the commandant was ordered to give scraps of lumber and waste wood to the poor. Actually, while all these shortages couldn't have improved tempers around Locke-Ober's tables, its effects on the health of the patrons was undoubtedly all to the good, although that rationalization probably wasn't a popular one at the time—especially since the grain crisis had led to the curtailment of the production of beer and distilled spirits.

The various restrictions of the war years were, as it turned out, only a prelude to what was to follow on their heels—Prohibition. Through the ceaseless efforts of the Prohibition party, the Woman's Christian Temperance Union, and most powerfully, the Anti-Saloon League, by 1917 twenty-six states had enacted prohibition laws, of which thirteen could be described as "bone dry." The arguments for prohibition had always appealed strongly to the country's large evangelical Protestant population for which the issue was primarily a moral one. Now it could be contended without too great a strain on the public credulity that it would not only keep the victims of alcohol from filling up the prisons and poorhouses, where they languished at public expense, but would actually help to win the war. By December, 1917, Congress had approved the prohibition resolution, within thirteen months it had been ratified by three-fourths of the states, and a year later it went into effect as the Eighteenth Amendment—the "Noble Experiment." Its effect on restaurants like Locke-Ober's was just short of disastrous.

The closing of the bars of course spelled doom for the operation of Locke's Wine Rooms at 1 and 2 Winter Place, which had to be abandoned. And since Camus, although naturally not in sympathy with the Prohibition Amendment, had no intention of operating outside the law—and indeed would have nothing to do with handling the kinds of liquors which were generally available in those days—the restaurant was forced to rely for survival solely on the quality of its food, the excellence of its service and the atmosphere in which the two were put together. This is not to claim that ardent spirits were never consumed on the premises. They were of course brought in by guests, more or less surreptitiously, parked close to table legs and mixed, more or less surreptitiously, with water, soda, ginger ale or whatever. In fact the discovery a few years ago of a large cache of empty bottles in a long-abandoned stair closet offered circumstantial evidence that an enterprising cashier of those days was operating quite a lucrative private concession while making change. Still, the restaurant itself sealed up its extensive wine cellar, tried to make the bar look as operative as possible and went on about the business of purveying fine food.

While the years of the Great Foolishness tended to

Looking down to the street level from the second-floor bar.

dampen many a spirit, an irrepressible one in the twenties belonged to Locke's very unofficial Director of Transportation, otherwise known as Freddie the Cabman who operated the last horse-dawn hack in Boston—in fact three hacks, depending on the weather: a victoria, a closed coach and a magnificent coupe on runners. Nobody ever knew how Freddie ferreted out social affairs but he never missed a debutante party, a waltz night or a club dinner, all the time attending to his specialty, the conveyance of Harvard men back to Cambridge at the end of their revels in Winter Place. The fare was $10.00, and Freddie who, it was commonly assumed, had not been completely sober for decades, appreciated it if his tip took the form of a bottle of S.S. Pierce's rum, transferred at the beginning of the trip. This naturally fortified Freddie against much inclement weather and made it possible for his riders to take the reins whenever they felt moved to do so. Even in those days Freddie was a survival piece whose silver side lamps were a symbol of the pleasures of the night. Alas, his like and occupation will not be looked upon again.

A decade later another act of God was to challenge the fortitude of the country's leading restaurants in the form of the Great Depression. And, unluckily, Prohibition and Depression were to overlap for more than three years, thus compounding their difficulties. By December, 1929, following the October debacle in Wall Street, three million people were unemployed; by the following winter that figure stood at somewhere between four and five million; and a year later it had reached a staggering eight million. At that point, the unemployment index leveled off but the Depression (presumably a less frightening word than "panic," although that is exactly what it was) continued right up to the beginning of the Second World War. Of this long grim period, ex-President Herbert

Hoover later said, it is hoped with some irony, "Many people left their jobs for the more profitable one of selling apples." This was the decade of the superfluous people and among them was the full quota of superfluous chefs, superfluous waiters and waitresses, superfluous restaurant owners because the American people were retrenching all along the line. They dropped their club memberships, they skipped vacations, they made fewer long-distance telephone calls, they bought fewer clothes, fewer flowers, fewer cuts of top-grade meat, and of course they patronized restaurants less frequently and, when they did, paid more attention to the price of each item on the menu.

It's hard for anyone under fifty to imagine it today but during the thirties at Locke-Ober's the price of Brook Trout Meunière hovered around $1.00; Chicken Sauté Parmentier (or Bordelaise, Chasseur, Viennoise or whatever) was $1.40; Porter House Steak *for two* was $4.50 and Lobster Savannah, the Specialty of the House, was $1.60! Yet there were people in those terrible days, some of whom had seen the inside of Locke-Ober's, who were managing to live on $1.60 a day.

Although the restaurant business remained generally sluggish all through the thirties, several events in 1933 and 1934 changed that dramatically for they led directly to the repeal of the Eighteenth Amendment. Popular disgust over the failure of enforcement of the Prohibition Amendment grew so steadily through the twenties and early thirties, partly as a by-product of the Depression, that the Democratic Convention in 1932—the same convention that nominated Franklin D. Roosevelt the first time—demanded its repeal, and the subsequent Democratic landslide in the November elections persuaded Congress that the time for action had come. In the short session (February 20, 1932), a resolution was approved to accomplish repeal. Submitted to the legislatures of the states, the Twenty-first Amendment was ratified in less than a year. But meanwhile, even before ratification, Congress on March 22, 1933, had legalized the sale of beverages containing not more than 3.2 percent alcohol, wherever state laws did not prohibit it. And although 3.2 percent meant essentially only beer, it was enough to open the bars—with considerable jubilation.

Thus ended the first experiment on the part of the American people in writing into the fundamental law of the land legislation attempting to regulate or control each other's personal habits. The liquor problem was turned back to the states. Emil Camus rejoiced along with many others. After all the difficult years since his wine cellar had been locked and his bars closed down, exacerbated by four long years of economic woes, he knew that his business would survive and prosper without sacrificing quality or abandoning tradition.

Camus continued to pilot Locke-Ober's for another half dozen years when he died on April 27, 1939, by an unusual coincidence, exactly thirty-eight years after he had assumed command for the second time in 1901. His impact on the establishment was, and to this day remains, profound. Although in 1978 there is only a single employee who actually worked under him, his name is mentioned frequently and always with respect. The systems he introduced, the service he insisted upon, the dishes he and his chefs perfected and introduced, the atmosphere he created—all these things persist as a kind of memorial to him which the present staff seems quietly determined to perpetuate unquestioningly. It all represents a kind of tribute he would of course have been extremely proud of.

Emil Camus had survived World War I, Prohibition and

the Great Depression and his death had at least spared him the problems that World War II brought with it. For restaurateurs like him it was a particularly challenging experience. Vastly increased numbers of citizens, flushed with artificial wartime prosperity, literally besieged restaurants like Locke-Ober's hoping to enjoy foods they were unable to come by in quantity or approximate in quality because of government rationing and miscellaneous shortages only to find their favorite eating places beset by the same conditions.

In April, 1941, it had been necessary for the government, by executive order, to set up the Office of Price Administration, thereafter always referred to as the OPA, whose task it was to ration food and control prices. Since the Philippines had been lost to the Japanese, the first casualty was sugar, which was rationed early in 1942. Sugar bowls then began to disappear from counters and tables and discreet signs were posted imploring customers not to take too much. Honey, molasses and saccharin were substituted in pastries, and desserts became comparatively Spartan.

Coffee, that sine qua non of the American diet, was allotted to the civilian population on the theoretical basis of one pound to a person every five weeks, so pots and second cups were discouraged.

The most sorely felt restriction was of course that of meat and, especially, beef. While by OPA decree GIs were allocated meat rations on the basis of 234 pounds annually and a Navy man, for some inexplicable reason, 364 pounds, civilians were expected to stay steamed up on only 140 pounds, and restaurants were required to estimate their consumption, based on previous experience, accordingly. An added deprivation for them and their patrons derived from the government's practice of requisitioning 60 percent of the prime cuts of meat available and 80 percent of the utility grades, thus leaving it to the better restaurants like Locke-Ober's to use more and more ingenuity in making inferior grades of meat palatable, observing meatless Tuesdays and Fridays, yielding to the temptation to deal with the black market, or greatly increasing their use of eggs and game. A few restaurants even experimented with horsemeat but never for long. Although disguised as much as possible—on the menu and on the stove—its sweetish flavor could not be made to appeal to American tastes.

Butter was another much prized rationed food and its near disappearance was greatly felt by Locke-Ober chefs who had always been liberal with its use in myriad dishes. (Its place was taken, at least on tables in private houses if seldom in restaurants, by margarine, which has continued to maintain its position as an honorable butter substitute ever since.)

Finally, even vegetables were rationed notwithstanding the 20,000,000 so-called victory gardens which quickly sprang up in town and country everywhere and before the war ended accounted for some 40 percent of all the vegetables the American people consumed. Among the items not actually rationed but often in short supply were milk and ice cream (when available, flavors were limited to eight) and beer and whiskey, the distillers having been persuaded to devote their talents to the production of industrial alcohol.

On a Locke-Ober dinner menu for 1943, it is interesting to note not a single offering of beef or pork—although, to be sure, this may have been a Tuesday or Friday menu. Instead there are nine different chicken and turkey dishes and four duck, and not suprisingly, fish and shellfish are dominant. During the war the cost of food in general rose 44 percent and this menu happens to bear that out precisely. Although the

Edward Ivaldi christening the new wine cellar in 1948.

famous Lobster Savannah, for instance, priced at $1.60 in the mid-thirties, was now a whopping $2.50! Where indeed are "the snows of yesteryear?" It was the Lobster Savannah, incidentally, which at odd times occupied the minds of unwilling expatriate New Englanders in those years. In 1945, ex-Sergeant William Kiley recalled that during the Battle of Bastogne, "we dreaded Christmas Day. We needn't have, though. It wasn't as blue as we feared it would be. We had something which was more than the Jerries had. We had K rations, heated—I drew pork loaf with apple flake, which isn't the ideal Christmas fare, but it was good. You'd never guess what we talked about that day. We all talked about what we'd eat when we got home and I just about drove everyone nuts talking about Lobster Savannah as served at Locke-Ober's."

If Kiley didn't paint the lily by selecting a wine to accompany his visionary Lobster Savannah, it was merely an oversight. Magny, the great Parisian restaurateur and epicure, said, "A good [wine] cellar can only be formed with the aid of time and prodigious faculties of taste." And he might have added, the proper storage facilities—constant temperature (58°–60° F.), controlled atmospheric conditions—not too dry —and bins or shelves so constructed that the bottles will never roll. Ever since the days when Louis Ober personally replenished his stock on periodic trips abroad, Locke-Ober's has been renowned for its cellar.

Now more than a hundred vintages, over two-thirds of them imported, are put down in an air-conditioned wine cellar constructed in 1948. Here the temperature and atmospheric conditions closely approximate those in the famous chalk tunnels, old stone quarries and deep catacombs of Reims which for years have served the champagne makers of France as ideal storage places for their wares. Here will be found the

95

red Bordeaux and Burgundies which traditionally accompany poultry, game, meat and cheese; the white Bordeaux and Burgundies to go with oysters, hors d'oeuvres, fish pâté and desserts; versatile Loire vintages which are such perfect accompaniments to hors d'oeuvres, meat, game, poultry, pâté and desserts; wines from Alsace and the Rhine country to enhance the enjoyment of oysters, hors d'oeuvres, fish and desserts; champagnes which perform ideally with any course except perhaps meat and game. And of course wine culture has so improved and flourished in the United States since World War II that representative American wines will be found here which rival and sometimes excel their European counterparts—for example, the red Cabernet Sauvignon and the white Chardonnay and Sauvignon Blanc. Even American champagnes are beginning to stand up to their French cousins.

A man can dine only once a day.

P. Z. DIDSBURY

ANY REMINISCENCE of Locke-Ober's during the war years and later forties reminds one of some of the durable personalities who entered its service in those days or, in one notable case, even earlier. Of these the dean of the waiter's staff is unquestionably Albert DiGiacomo who must have been a very young man when he came aboard in 1930 because his energy at this writing is prodigious. Albert has seen them come and go for forty-eight years and they intimidate him not, yet his desire to aid and abet his customers' idiosyncracies and gustatory pleasures is obviously as keen as ever.

Frank Curro, sometimes irreverently referred to as "Frankie," and now headwaiter in the downstairs dining room, signed on late in 1942. Frank began his working career at the ill-fated Coconut Grove night club and when that was destroyed in the terrible fire that killed 491 people in November that year, he transferred to Locke-Ober's first as a general

One of seven private dining rooms on the third floor.

handyman, then busboy, and successively counterman, waiter, captain and finally headwaiter. His duties often demand a knowledge, firmness and diplomacy that would challenge the State Department's Chief of Protocol and he performs them with élan.

Another fugitive from the Coconut Grove is Adolf Cecchini who for many years has presided as headwaiter on the second and third floors. "Chico," as he is familiarly known, came to Boston from Italy at the age of sixteen, worked at the old Touraine Hotel, the Copley Plaza and the Ritz-Carlton and also settled in at Locke's late in 1942 where he has over the years become a kind of movable symbol of the Locke-Ober tradition.

No patron of the (then) men's dining room between 1945 and 1967 will forget the elegant style with which "Freddie" Hammel glided hither and yon greeting and seating customers and directing the service crew. Tall, suave, impeccably turned out in striped trousers, black jacket and pearl gray tie, with an impish humor and a twinkling eye, Freddie was the perfect host. There were times, though, when he could be uncompromising when stung. In the fall of 1967, when the curator of the Nieman Foundation at Harvard brought a group of the Fellows to Locke's and one of them ordered a Gibson, a martini with an onion rather than an olive in it, Freddie announced with some finality that the Gibson had been stricken from the beverage list. The reason for the ban was learned later: Bob Gibson, the St. Louis Cardinals pitcher, had just beaten the Boston Red Sox in the final game of the World Series, and obviously Freddie believed in making the punishment fit the crime. In due time he agreed to take over the direction of the third-floor private dining rooms but finally wearied of that comparatively restrained atmosphere and exchanged it for outright retirement.

Early in 1946, Reno Masciocchi, who, incidentally, had also survived the Coconut Grove fire, joined the other alumni at Locke-Ober's. Now second in command in the second-floor dining rooms, he is always in the right place at the right time, always able to solve a problem, and never surprised when things go right.

On the management level, since the death of the legendary Emil Camus, two individuals have left their marks on the establishment. Charles W. Little and William Harrington flourished, shall we say, for twenty-eight and twenty-seven years respectively, which, if nothing else, speaks well for the food. Each man regarded his job as a kind of inheritance. Both sought to maintain traditional standards and procedures. (Little once said, "Locke-Ober's must remain unchanging in this changing world. Our customers demand this of us, so we have no choice but to comply.") Obviously their stewardship had much to do with carrying Locke's up to and into its second century.

The "names" who have been welcomed and served, often again and again, by these able, even dedicated professionals would read like a *Who's Who* (and *Who Was Who*) *in America*. And it would be as impossible to mention, say, all those Bostonians, famous and infamous, of recent years who have been Locke-Ober habitués as it would be to list those among them who have seen Faneuil Hall. With perhaps two or three exceptions. When John F. Kennedy lunched at Locke's, he invariably had a proposition for Frank Curro which was of course never rejected. He would propose that he and Frank share a Lobster Stew (page 131), which involved his drinking the broth and Frank eating the meat, after which JFK usually addressed a steak.

100

Caricature of Huntington R. ("Tack") Hardwick, in a Harvard alumni paper of 1936, when he was an eight-letter man, with three in football, three in baseball and two in track.

Another charming bit of history concerns Huntington F. ("Tack") Hardwick, sometime Harvard all-American football great and later a Boston investment banker and broker who lunched almost daily in Winter Place while bent over a crossword puzzle. The day following his death in 1949, the plate was turned down on his customary table and a bottle of his favorite wine, an antique pepper mill and the day's crossword puzzle were put at his place.

A Bostonian who was one of Locke's fiercest partisans—and his partisanship was generally fierce—was the columnist and literary gadfly, George Frazier. George may be said to have embellished Locke-Ober's with his English tailoring and usual boutonniere, and it will be remembered that he appropriated and Americanized the Spanish word *duende*, meaning style or class. For him there were only two kinds of persons and institutions: those who had *duende* and those utterly lacking it. Locke-Ober's, he thought, had *duende*, and he attested to it in a long article in *Holiday* magazine in 1951—one of the best pieces George ever wrote.

Among those who have made recurring pilgrimages to Locke-Ober's from the hinterlands, a special case must be Lucius Beebe. Beebe, for those who have forgotten or are too young to remember, was a sartorially elegant bon vivant, writer, raconteur, epicure and wine connoisseur (of an operation he survived, a friend said, "No doubt they'll open Lucius at room temperature"), and exponent of every phase of the life beautiful whose plangent prose enriched newspapers, magazines and books during the thirties, forties and fifties and who kept returning as one possessed to the amenities of Locke-Ober's. These visits he was in the habit of celebrating in magazines like *Gourmet*, the old *Pageant*, his book *Boston and the Boston Legend* and a syndicated column in the late lamented *New York Herald Tribune*. One of his appreciations ends thusly: "Locke's has no peer and few rivals. And the top-hatted ghosts at its bar are those great of the legendary past: Eben Jordan and Theodore Roosevelt, John Drew and Dr. Lowell. They are all drinking Ward Eights with Nick (Stuhl) and Mr. Camus and the founding fathers, Locke and Ober." You know, Lucius, you might just be right.

One of the most original versifiers in all of American letters was also a confirmed devotee of Locke's. He was the late Ogden Nash who couldn't have agreed more with a newspaper columnist's comment that undertaking a trip to Boston without visiting Locke-Ober's would be like going to Agra and ignoring the Taj Mahal. On his frequent commutes between his winter home in Baltimore and his summer place at Rye Beach, New Hampshire, lunch or dinner at Locke's was a veritable rite of passage. At these occasions one might have logically assumed that Ogden was on a fairly strict regiment known as the Martini and Lobster Diet consisting of two martinis, straight up, and a boiled lobster (the traditional New England treatment) of at least passable size. So far as is known, the regal lobster never inspired Ogden's lyric genius —as the lowly turtle did, which he described as living "twixt plated decks"—but he was moved to song about the martini in a verse which goes:

> *There is something about a Martini,*
> *A tingle remarkably pleasant*
> *A yellow, a mellow Martini;*
> *I wish that I had one at present.*
> *There is something about a Martini,*
> *Ere the dining and dancing begin,*
> *And to tell you the truth,*
> *It is not the vermouth—*
> *I think that perhaps it's the gin.*

As the martini inspired Ogden Nash, the Tom Collins— or rather, a variation thereof—apparently inspired the actor Edward Everett Horton who in retrospect one can imagine as building an entire career in the ever popular *Springtime for Henry*. Whenever *he* dined at Locke's, so various is the human species, he invariably took a Tom Collins or two into which he ordered submerged a couple of cucumber spears. One can only wonder how a combination of such ingredients could possibly have been arrived at. In an experimental laboratory perhaps? By some bizarre and unimaginable accident? By this time we shall never know and, in any case, "to each his own."

Jack Benny, belying his public image as the stingiest man in the world, invariably appeared at Locke's whenever he was in Boston. His respect for the restorative powers of the martini rivaled Poet Nash's and a ritual always accompanied the drinking of two, straight up, which he ordered served together. Arranging one behind the other before him, he proceeded to sip No. 2 first, which usually provoked a "Why?" from a naturally curious waiter. "Because," he would blandly explain, "the second one goes down so much easier than the first." Incontrovertible.

Two other great entertainment figures have been less easily charmed at Locke's. Danny Kaye, not entirely satisfied with a dish he ordered, once advanced on the kitchen and proceeded to prepare his own meal, all the while performing snatches of one of his song-and-dance routines, to the exquisite delight of the entire kitchen staff.

Peter Lorre, the lachrymose Hungarian, apparently conducted a lifelong quest for goulash the way they put it together in Budapest. And when he found goulash on the menu, one had the impression he ordered it only to prove to himself again—with expressions of resigned disdain—that nobody in North America can create goulash as any third-rate cook is capable of doing in Hungary.

Yes, Locke's has had its share of guests who were and are originals. Such was Elsa Maxwell—doyenne of party arrangers, companion of the rich, famous and titled, a genuine social phenomenon. She was, incidentally, a contemporary of Lucius

Locke-Ober's special "Menu du Mercredi 12 Octobre 1949"—
commemorating the arrival of the Ile de France *in Boston.*

Beebe and one might say they had many of the same clients. When her memoirs, *R.S.V.P., Elsa Maxwell's Own Story*, were published by Little, Brown and Company in 1954, what better place to celebrate the event than at the Locke-Ober Café. The occasion, though, turned out to be not without its peculiar complications. To be a bit personal, Elsa was on the portly side to say the least, a fact of life which for her had long made stairways exquisitely irrelevant. And unfortunately her publisher in all innocence had arranged his party for a private dining room on the restaurant's third floor. Delivered to the door by limousine, Miss Maxwell was immediately appalled to discover what appeared to be a formidable flight of stairs confronting her, whereupon she promptly declared she would go no farther. Here was an obvious social crisis. Finally, after much cajolery, Elsa agreed to proceed upward if her accompanying editor would get behind and push. Which he did, albeit inelegantly and with considerable apprehension that if the whole maneuver failed, he ran the risk of being crushed like an eggshell. But all went well as far as the second floor where Elsa, breathlessly, asked to be shown her table, only to be told it was still another flight up. This announcement, although made as tactfully as possible in the circumstances, provoked another outcry which most of the diners in the vicinity were privy to. At last, however, the party proceeded gradually upward, Elsa's companion supplying as much power as he could for each step and backstopping the chief performer when that was reached. The luncheon, it might be said, went off as well as could be expected in view of its inauspicious beginnings, largely due to the excellence of the food and drink. It might only be added that as mountain climbers know, descending a mountain is almost as perilous as the ascent.

Locke-Ober Cafe

Harvard-Army
Dinner

SATURDAY
OCTOBER 21, 1950

An example of a special menu cover in the fifties.

Actually over the years Locke-Ober's has seen so many notables pass through its doors that a certain sense of the inevitable about them long ago set in, the expectation that they will inevitably appear from time to time, that they will be served with the same expertise as that accorded any other guest, no more and no less, and that they will in all probability go out to become ambassadors for the restaurant for all time. While no formal record of a diner is kept, the staff can't help but remember (in addition to the inevitable Bostonians) such comparatively recent guests, and diverse personalities, as Adlai Stevenson, Averell Harriman, Roberta Peters, Ginger Rogers, John Glenn, Helen Hayes, Boris Karloff, Ted Williams, Van Cliburn, Peter Ustinov, Norman Mailer, Jimmy Durante, Ezio Pinza, Charles Laughton, Casey Stengel, James Beard, Robert Merrill, Joan Crawford, Marilyn Monroe and Joe DiMaggio—to name a mere handful. Yet it should be emphasized that Locke's survives not because it is a place to see and be seen. It survives for a more basic reason which must have been that of the founders—to serve the Boston community. If it also happens to serve the community's guests, well and good.

Cooking is like love. It should be entered into with abandon or not at all.

HARRIET VAN HORNE

THE THIRD-FLOOR dining rooms at Locke's, as well as the handsome, and larger, Ober Room on the second floor have been the scenes of many memorable private dining entertainments over the years. But none perhaps have been more distinguished than the semiannual gathering one evening in May, 1965, of some forty members of The Beefeater Club of the Incorporated Ancient Order of The Beefeater. Founded in London after World War II as an organization designed "to promote good fellowship and to perpetuate the ancient British tradition of good living, loyalty and friendship," in 1953 the New York headquarters was established by Mr. R. C. Kopf, the present Governor, to further this tradition of goodwill, to enlarge it by an emphasis on Britain's contribution to gastronomy and to extend it by placing an important consideration

THE BEEFEATER MARTINI

MENU

WELLFLEET OYSTERS
CHINCOTEAGUE OYSTERS

GRAACHER HIMMELREICH SPATLESE 1961
FUDER No. 38 ORIG. ABF. JOH. JOS. PRUM

CONSOMME STRASBOURGEOIS

MOUSSE OF DOVER SOLE CHURCHILL

CHATEAU CHEVAL BLANC 1960
(SAINT EMILION)

SWEETBREADS WITH ALMONDS

BEAUNE BOUCHEROTTES 1961
ESTATE BOTTLED BY LOUIS JADOT

RACK OF SPRING LAMB SAIGNANT

ANGLO-FRENCH CHEESE PLATTER

TAITTINGER BRUT-LA FRANCAISE
EN MAGNUM

AMERICAN WILD STRAWBERRIES

LARRESSINGLE
"RESERVE TRESOR" ARMAGNAC

DEMITASSE OF MOCHA
AND JAVA COFFEE

DETTLING KIRSCHWASSER

CHEF DE CUISINE - MARTIN MANZONETTA.

*In May, 1965, The Beefeater Club of the Incorporated Ancient Order
of The Beefeater convened at Locke-Ober for a "Banquet in the
Eastern Bailiwick." This is the salient part of the menu for that
unusual gustatory event.*

Fortified by their repast in the old Ober Room, The Beefeaters proceed to the installation of new members.

on charitable aims—since the annual dues of some thousand members in the United States are funneled into qualified philanthropic organizations by way of a Beefeater foundation.

Although it is said that Alexander Dumas produced the magic number nine as the maximum for a perfect dinner, The Beefeaters have found from experience that about forty male diners will not make cohesion a problem in the right setting, a fairly intimate room, and that almost any fine restaurant or hotel can accommodate that number without sacrificing the kind of food, drink and service required by the tastes and traditions of The Beefeaters.

On pages 110 and 111 there is reproduced the menu of The Beefeater dinner at Locke-Ober's together with accompanying beverages, including what the popular English writer Alec Waugh called "the perfect *preparatif*," a Beefeater Martini—of which The Beefeaters invariably limit themselves to one. (Incidentally, any Beefeater observing a fellow member who is not wearing the official Beefeater tie on Wednesdays is entitled to demand a Beefeater Martini of the miscreant. It would seem that a no more appropriate penalty could be found to fit the crime.) After the festivities on that May evening in '65, when an Officer asked the assemblage whether the traditions of The Beefeater Club had been honored by the dinner, they responded to a man by calling out, "Tout va bien," the Beefeater lingua franca indicating general approval of Chef Martin Manzonetta's creations.

It might be noted that a recipe for Mousse of Dover Sole Cardinal may be found on page 147, two for Sweetbreads on pages 171 and 172, and one for a Rack of Lamb, properly pink, on page 175.

In 1974 the room The Beefeaters had used, the Ober Room, underwent a major transformation which Louis Ober would surely have approved. When the building formerly occupied by the Columbia National Life Insurance Company, around the corner on Franklin Street, was remodeled, it was learned that the quartered oak paneling in a Directors' Room, of about the Ober Room's dimensions, would be available. It had been designed and meticulously carved by artisans of Irving and Casson, which had become the successors to the famous furniture makers A. H. Davenport and Company, and Locke's manager at the time, Bill Harrington, lost no time in acquiring it. The result, as adapted to the Ober Room, is a decor which approaches the richness and intricacy of detail of the dining room downstairs and which typifies the turn-of-the-century era of which it is a noble survivor.

Somewhat earlier, in fact in the early fifties, the second floor of what had been Frank Locke's Wine Rooms was reacquired and after extensive remodeling became the Camus Room, a name which, alas, in these later days sometimes requires identification.

The second-floor Ober Room.

Strange to see how a good dinner and feasting reconciles everybody.

SAMUEL PEPYS

AUGUST 26, 1970, dawned like any other Wednesday at the Locke-Ober Café in Boston—refuse cans were elevated to the street, deliverymen whistled as they shuttled in and out, the cat came back—but before it ended, a sacred precinct (in fact, a damned sacred precinct) was to be invaded, sensibilities were to be outraged, a ninety-five-year tradition was to be flouted, the raw power of 53 percent of the human race was to be flaunted. Female persons were to lunch in the heretofore exclusive men's dining room, brazenly, smugly, obliviously and, evidently, quite happily. Until that fateful day, ladies (if not women) had been permitted to dine with their escorts in the ground-floor dining room, in full view of the pedestrians in Winter Place, on two occasions a year, New Year's Eve and the evening of the Harvard-Yale football game—generally referred to locally as a classic.

But in the summer of 1970, it will be recalled, the winds of social change were blowing even in Boston, blowing so briskly, in fact, that an intrepid young woman at the Massachusetts Institute of Technology telephoned Locke-Ober's and, using the name Dr. Remington, which happened to be her own, engaged a table for lunch on Wednesday for a party of eight. When the group arrived it was first met with indulgent smiles by the diners already seated, but when it became clear Dr. Remington was *the* Dr. Remington and clearly meant business, Headwaiter Frank Curro sagaciously decided to go along with the joke. The rest is history. Nowadays, actually, the fun of liberating Locke's street-level dining room over and over again at lunchtime has largely worn off and the men are perforce again usually left alone to talk about whatever it is men talk about when there are no female people around to distract them. At the dinner hour, though, it's an entirely different story. Then there will be found a marked prevalence of women in the former sanctum sanctorum, which seems to have suffered no visible evidence of defilement as a result. And there are those even who believe that *Mademoiselle Yvonne* now appears to be raising her goblet in a somewhat freer attitude.

After all, why should Locke-Ober's not have taken the women into its arms? For a hundred years and more in Boston it has been a kind of Universal Aunt, though dispensing much more than sugar cookies, whenever an event or a situation suggests the mutual enjoyment of food. Births and birthdays, anniversaries, graduations, reunions, weddings, divorces, retirements, promotions, homecomings, departures, elections, sporting contests—almost everything has been celebrated here or at least solemnized. In fact, "household word" comes to mind in connection with the place. For example, not long ago

Town and Country magazine reported that "the opening of the recent television series *The Adams Chronicles* brought together dozens of Adams descendants to watch the portrayal. 'It was scary,' an invited nonfamily member said. 'They nodded and joked about everything Abigail Adams said on the tube as if they were going to lunch with her the next day at Locke-Ober.' " Abigail Adams at Locke-Ober? Considering the disparity in their ages, the thought is a little hard to get used to; still, had it been possible, Abigail and Locke's would not have intimidated one another.

In a way, too, the things Locke's furnishes has become a common medium of exchange in certain circles. In former societies money has been variously represented by stones, shells, ivory, wampum beads, tobacco and even dried fish. But in our more sophisticated civilization one is not surprised to overhear, as one did, a well-known member of the Massachusetts legislature saying to another, "I'll bet you a dinner at Locke-Ober's, with champagne, that you can't get that bill through the House this session."

And for foreign visitors—by which is meant anyone outside the confines of the six New England states— Locke-Ober's is one of the primary alternatives to dining and entertaining, as the French logically say, *en famille*. Recently, for instance, for Princess Grace of Monaco, the Ober Room provided just the right setting for dinner, partly because it is somewhat larger than the average dining room in a private house and much, much smaller than a hall, but principally because it was thought the meal—chilled cucumber soup, rack of lamb, Bibb lettuce, endive and sliced orange salad, strawberries in a crown-shaped patty shell, California wine and dry champagne—would (and by all reports did) leave the princess feeling perfectly serene.

117

This is an adjunct to the Locke-Ober story. In 1947, Cleveland Amory, in *The Proper Bostonians*, referred to a certain Monsieur Josef as Boston's "No. 1 Society restaurateur," with headquarters on the corner of Dartmouth and Newbury Streets in Boston's Back Bay. Monsieur Josef, he claimed, had "long enjoyed a high reputation for his ability to tell the right people from the wrong people" and "his ability appears to rest on his readily offered opinion that when the right people gather at dinner they will agree on the same choice of food and that the wrong people will all order differently"—a tantalizing observation the significance of which, if any, must be left to the sociologists. In any case, the pertinent fact was that in 1949, after the death of the Monsieur, the Locke-Ober Company took his restaurant—within walking distance of some of the city's finest hotels—anglicized its name to "Joseph's," made certain changes in the decor which would increase its appeal to men and operates it to this day with the same menu and on the same principles as those obtaining in Winter Place.

Alexis De Tocqueville, one of Europe's shrewdest observers of the American scene, said a century and a half ago, "Americans consider society as a body in a state of improvement in which nothing is, or ought to be, permanent." He was largely but not wholly correct. While Americans are quite willing to accept, indeed to welcome, improvements in almost anything touching their daily lives, there remain certain rituals which they prefer to be unchanging. Among these is the preparation, serving and savoring of fine foods. This sense of permanence, of dependability, of esteem for quality, of attention to detail, of awareness of the importance of a distinctive ambiance pervades all too few public dining places in this country, and for obvious reasons. After all, only a handful of them flourishing today had the good fortune to begin their

lives as early as 1875, at just about the beginning of the Gilded
Age. That was a time when carved mahogany, decorated ceilings, flocked wallpaper, brass-studded leather, stained glass,
gas lighting, gleaming silver and polished brass were common
elements of the internal decor of public places. It was also a
time when standards of painstaking excellence were handed
down from generation to generation of workers in kitchens
and dining rooms—the inclination, for instance, to obtain the
finest ingredients available, the habit of cooking every dish to
order, the ability to make patrons feel like guests rather than
mere casual customers, finally, the cultivation of the attitude
that satisfying dining may perhaps be the only truly lasting
pleasure in life. Many restaurants with great names have disappeared because, through overconfidence or after a change
of management, they forgot that the maintenance of standards is a daily struggle. Of those that have survived, some have
deservedly become virtual institutions. Locke-Ober Café in
Boston continues to be such a one.

Locke-Ober sign. The identifying sign over the entrance in Winter Place, heavy with symbolism and nineteenth-century scrollwork.

That all softening overpowering knell,
The tocsin of the soul—the dinner bell.

BYRON

A POTPOURRI

ON THE following pages will be found the recipes for various dishes featured at Locke-Ober Café. Quite obviously no attempt has been made to make this a "balanced" list. On the contrary, it is highly idiosyncratic, reflecting the tastes and specialties of the restaurant's various chefs and even the interests of the authors. It should, though, be reiterated here that the recipes in themselves embody no magical cooking procedures but reflect, rather, the culinary traditions to which Locke-Ober's has held fast for over a century—the use of the freshest of ingredients, the uniformly high quality thereof and, above all, the utmost care in preparation.

OYSTERS À LA GINO
(SERVES 4)

Oysters were relished by the Indians of all the American coasts eons before the white man became addicted to them, as hundreds of excavated middens bear witness. But it was in the latter half of the nineteenth century that oyster consumption reached its peak per capita—before the widespread pollution of the natural breeding grounds and after railroad transportation became dependable on a national scale, making it possible to ship oysters (and clams) packed in ice or saltwater-soaked hay. While oysters may be prepared in dozens of ways, purists insist that only raw oysters on the half shell—with a bit of lemon juice or some fresh horseradish and a few drops of Tabasco—are truly the food of the gods. From the 1860s until World War II, oyster bars, like the one maintained to this day in Locke's downstairs dining room, were an integral part of fine restaurants and hotels and oyster "parlors" dotted the landscape, offering primarily oysters on the half shell and oyster stew. Americans still consume respectable quantities of Bluepoints, Chincoteagues, Cotuits, Lynnhavens, Olympias and many more varieties, but in comparatively modest quantities per person. In former times two or three dozen fat oysters on the half shell with a bottle of beer, ale or dry white wine was just the normal appetizer before the soup.

Some thirty years ago Chef Gino Bertolaccini, in an experimental mood, invented this variation on Oysters Rockefeller and it has been a popular standby on Locke's menu ever since.

122

First Step

4 raw, lean bacon strips	1¼ cups cream sauce (page
1 clove garlic	193)
2 cups fresh crabmeat	¼ cup Madeira wine
2 teaspoons paprika	Salt and pepper

Mince together the bacon and the garlic. Fry until the bacon is crisp, drain off the fat. Blend the bacon and garlic mixture with the crabmeat and paprika. Fold in cream sauce and Madeira. Salt and pepper to taste. Bring to a quick boil, pour into a shallow pan and cool.

Second Step

1 clove garlic	Rock salt
1½ cups fresh bread crumbs	24 large oysters
¼ cup olive oil	6–8 strips raw, lean bacon
2 teaspoons paprika	

Mince the garlic and mix with the bread crumbs, olive oil and paprika (enough to color the mixture a rich red). Cover four ovenproof plates with a layer of rock salt and place 6 large, opened oysters on the half shell in each dish.

Place a generous mound of the reserved crabmeat mixture on each oyster and then sprinkle on a layer of the breadcrumb mixture. Top each oyster with a small curl of raw bacon. Place in a 375-degree oven and bake about 15 minutes or until bacon is crisp and the crumb topping is brown. Serve at once with lemon wedges.

BAKED OYSTERS BALLARD
(SERVES 6)

7 cloves fresh garlic	20 slices white bread, crusts removed
1½ teaspoons Spanish paprika	¼ cup chopped parsley
½ teaspoon white pepper	¼ cup olive oil
¾ pound salted butter	36 large oysters
	Rock salt

Mince 6 cloves of the garlic and blend well with 1 teaspoon of the paprika, pepper and butter. Roll in wax paper and refrigerate overnight.

Rub bread through a colander, or place in a blender at high speed until very fine; mince the remaining garlic clove and add to the bread crumbs with the ½ teaspoon of paprika, the parsley and olive oil.

Open oysters, discarding flat shell; sprinkle lightly with bread-crumb mixture. Slice butter mixture into ¼-inch slices and place 1 slice on each oyster. Put rock salt in six ovenproof baking dishes and place 6 oysters on rock salt in each dish. (This process helps to hold the heat once the oysters are removed from the oven and prevents their rolling, hence losing butter.) Bake in a 375-degree oven until well browned (10 to 12 minutes).

BAKED CLAMS CASINO
(SERVES 4.)

32 Little Neck clams on the half shell
2 cups finely rubbed fresh bread crumbs
2 teaspoons paprika
1 clove of garlic, chopped fine
¼ cup olive oil
8 bacon strips

Put 8 clams into each of four heatproof baking dishes. Mix together bread crumbs, paprika, garlic and oil, and divide the mixture among the clams. Place a generous strip of bacon on each one. Put in a 350-degree oven and cook until bacon is crisp. Serve with lemon wedges.

CANAPÉ MARTHA
(SERVES 4.)

2 tablespoons butter
1 pound fresh lobster meat, cut in large cubes
2 teaspoons paprika
¼ cup sherry wine
1 cup cream sauce (page 193)
4 slices white toast
Cheese sauce (page 195)
4 tablespoons grated Parmesan cheese

Melt butter in saucepan, add lobster and paprika and cook until lobster is heated through. Add sherry wine and cook slowly about 5 minutes. Add cream sauce and stir until mixture is well blended. Place a piece of toast in each of four individual heatproof dishes and then spoon lobster mixture over it. Cover lobster mixture with a thin layer of cheese sauce, dust top with fresh Parmesan cheese and brown under the broiler.

ESCARGOTS BOURGUIGNONNE
(APPETIZERS FOR 8)

Two things militate against a more universal enjoyment of snails: for some people they are not particularly attractive little creatures when met with in the garden, and the method of extracting them can be intimidating—manipulating the small tongs that grip the shell while picking out the edible morsel with a short, two-pronged fork. If, though, these obstacles can be overcome, the snail—brown and hot and rich with butter and a touch of garlic—is an unforgettable taste sensation.

2 pounds butter	2 tablespoons chopped parsley
6–8 cloves fresh garlic, chopped fine	3 ounces chicken broth
48 snails (2 large cans) with shells	¼ cup Madeira wine
	½ teaspoon salt

Place butter in sauté pan and cook until it begins to turn brown. Add chopped garlic and sauté until light brown. Add snails and sauté for approximately 1 minute. Add parsley, chicken broth, Madeira and salt. Cook until liquid is reduced about ¼. Place a little of the sauce in each shell, then add a snail. Reserve remaining sauce. Be sure to use a large shell for a large snail. Place in a 425-degree oven long enough to get very hot. Pour reserved sauce over snails and serve.

ANCHOVIES, WINTER PLACE
(SERVES 4)

Mixed greens
52 anchovy fillets
1 large onion, chopped fine
8 slices of tomato

1 hard boiled egg, chopped fine
French dressing (page 203)

Arrange the mixed greens in an oval on four medium-sized salad plates. On each bed of greens arrange 13 anchovy fillets in a lattice design. Place chopped onion on one side of greens and 2 slices of tomato on the other. Sprinkle chopped egg over the top of the anchovies. Serve with Locke-Ober's French dressing.

EGGS FISHERMAN
(SERVES 4)

Boston lettuce
1½ pounds fresh crabmeat
6 cold hard boiled eggs, split in half

1 cup mayonnaise (page 202)
6 stuffed olives, sliced
16 slices tomato

Garnish four large salad plates with Boston lettuce. Divide crabmeat among the plates and shape into long, narrow mounds. Place 3 hard boiled egg halves, flat side down, on each portion. Cover each egg with a generous spoonful of mayonnaise and place a slice of olive on each egg half. Arrange 4 slices tomato on each plate and serve.

COLD EGG VICTORIA
(SERVES 4)

Mixed salad greens
1½ cups mayonnaise (page 202)
¾ cup unsweetened whipped cream

1 pound lobster meat, cut in large cubes
8 cold poached eggs
16 slices tomato

Arrange mixed greens in an oval shape on four plates. Mix mayonnaise and whipped cream. Mix lobster meat with ¼ to ⅓ of the mayonnaise and cream dressing. Divide equally over top of greens. Place 2 poached eggs on top of each mound. Cover with remaining dressing. Garnish each plate with sliced tomatoes.

EGGS BENEDICT
(SERVES 4)

8 English muffin halves
8 slices Canadian Bacon
8 eggs

Hollandaise sauce (page 201)
Eight ½-inch cuts of truffle

Toast English muffins, grill bacon and poach eggs. Arrange two muffin halves on each of four hot ovenproof plates. Top with 2 slices of grilled bacon and 2 poached eggs. Mask with Hollandaise sauce and garnish with truffles. Place in a 325-degree oven for 2 minutes. Serve hot.

After a good dinner, one can forgive any-body, even one's own relatives.

OSCAR WILDE

NEW ENGLAND FISH CHOWDER
(MAKES APPROXIMATELY 2 QUARTS)

1½ pounds haddock
1 large onion, chopped
¼ cup ground salt pork
2 quarts fish stock (page 198)
½ cup flour ⎫
4 ounces butter ⎭ roux

2 cups light cream, heated
3 large potatoes, peeled, diced and cooked in stock
Salt
White pepper

Simmer haddock for 20 minutes in stock, flake and hold in reserve.

Sauté onion in the salt pork until it turns the color of straw, about 5 minutes. Add the fish stock, let simmer for ½ hour, then thicken with roux. Simmer an additional 30 minutes and strain. Add hot cream to chowder, then potatoes and the flaked fish. Salt and pepper to taste.

LOBSTER BISQUE
(MAKES 2 GENEROUS QUARTS)

2 live chicken lobsters
½ cup cooking oil
2 stalks celery, diced
1 medium onion, diced
1 large carrot, diced
1 clove garlic, crushed
½ cup flour
3 tablespoons paprika

4 tablespoons tomato puree
1½ teaspoons salt
1 teaspoon pepper
2 quarts hot fish stock (page 198)
3 tablespoons butter
Light cream to add to base

Cut lobsters in half, detach claws and crack. Heat cooking oil in a large pot almost to smoking point. Add lobsters and braise until slightly pink. Add celery, onion, carrot and garlic. Continue to cook until vegetables are slightly brown. Add flour and cook, stirring continuously, until well blended. Add paprika, tomato purée, salt and pepper. Add hot stock slowly and stir until well blended. Reduce to a low heat and simmer slowly for 2 hours. Pass this base through a fine strainer and, if not serving immediately, dot the surface of the soup with butter to keep a skin from forming. Reserve lobster meat separately. To finish soup use ⅔ base to ⅓ hot light cream. Dice lobster meat and add to soup when serving.

LOBSTER STEW
(SERVES 4.)

1½ pounds cooked lobster
    knuckle meat
4 ounces butter (preferably
    sweet)

1 pint light cream
1 pint milk
  Salt and pepper

Sauté lobster meat in 3 ounces sweet butter until meat is firm. Add light cream and milk and bring just to a boil. Be careful not to boil. Add salt and pepper to taste. Remove from heat and ladle into soup tureen. Float 1 ounce sweet butter on top and serve immediately with pilot crackers. (The stew has more flavor if it is allowed to set for 24 hours, then reheated just to boiling.)

NEW ENGLAND CLAM CHOWDER
(MAKES APPROXIMATELY 2 QUARTS)

First Step

12 quahogs—wash well to remove sand
2 stalks celery, diced
1 medium onion, diced
½ clove garlic, minced

1 small bay leaf
¼ cup parsley stems
1½ quarts cold water
1 cup diced raw potatoes

Place all ingredients except potatoes in stockpot and simmer slowly for 20 minutes. Remove quahogs and cool. Pass stock through a fine strainer. Add potatoes to stock and cook slowly until potatoes are tender.

Second Step

2 ounces ground salt pork
1 small onion, cut in small dice
1 stalk celery, cut in small dice

1 leek, cut in small dice
¼ cup flour
Light cream, scalded
Salt and pepper

Place salt pork, onion, celery and leek in saucepan and cook slowly until vegetables are tender. Add flour and simmer for 5 minutes; add hot stock and potatoes and blend; continue to simmer for 15 minutes.

Open cooked clams and separate necks and stomachs, cut stomachs in small pieces, put necks through a food grinder and add to stock and potatoes. To finish the chowder, use ⅔ base to ⅓ scalded cream. Salt and pepper to taste.

VICHYSSOISE
(MAKES APPROXIMATELY 1½ QUARTS)

Vichyssoise, now on practically every restaurant menu worthy of the name, is the sophisticated cousin of a traditional French peasant soup. It was originated early in this century by Louis Diat, well-known chef at the Ritz-Carlton in New York.

Base

3 tablespoons butter
1 medium Spanish onion, diced
2 leeks (white part only) cut in large pieces
¼ cup chopped watercress stems
3 tablespoons flour

1 quart rich chicken broth
4 cups diced raw potatoes
Salt
White pepper
1 pinch (generous) nutmeg
½ tablespoon chopped fresh tarragon

Add

Light cream   Chives

Melt the butter in a large pot. Add onion, leeks and watercress stems. Cook until onions are transparent (do not brown). Add flour and blend well. Stir in hot chicken stock, add potatoes and simmer slowly for 30 minutes. Add salt, pepper, nutmeg and chopped tarragon and simmer slowly for 1 hour. Strain this base through a medium colander. Press with a ladle to properly force potatoes and as much pulp as possible through colander. Chill in refrigerator. To finish, use 2 parts base to 1 part light cream. Mix well and put through fine strainer. Serve in cups and top with chopped chives.

Can be heated if desired.

*In comparison with the stars, what is more
trifling a matter than my dinner?*

ST. AUGUSTINE

COPENHAGEN LOBSTER PLATE
(SERVES 4)

Boston lettuce leaves
2 pounds fresh lobster meat
16 fresh or canned asparagus tips (white Belgian preferably)
4 tomatoes, quartered

8 small fillets of salmon (divide into 16 long strips)
1 teaspoon curry powder
3 tablespoons sherry wine
2 cups mayonnaise (page 202)

Garnish four luncheon-size plates with Boston lettuce leaves. Arrange 4 mounds of lobster meat on the outer perimeter of each plate. Place asparagus tips and tomato wedges between the mounds of lobster. Top asparagus tips with smoked salmon strips.

Place curry powder in a mixing bowl, add sherry and blend well. Mix in mayonnaise, divide the sauce into four small glass or china cups. Place a cup in the middle of each plate. Serve chilled.

134

LOBSTER AND SHRIMP AMÉRICAINE
(SERVES 2)

What makes a dish "à la Américaine?" In this case, the flavoring of the distinctive American tomato would seem to be the answer.

2 tablespoons mirepoix*	One 1-pound can tomatoes
½ pound fresh lobster meat, cut in large dice	chopped fine (reserve liquid)
1 pound raw shrimp, without their shells	6 tablespoons sherry wine
	Chopped parsley

Place mirepoix, lobster and shrimp in sauté pan and heat. Add tomatoes and sherry. Add ½ the liquid from tomatoes and simmer gently for 10 minutes. Add generous pinch of chopped parsley. Serve very hot on crisp toast.

* Mirepoix: This flavoring mixture for stews, soups and sauces was supposedly named after a French duke of the time of Louis XV.

½ small carrot, chopped fine	1 bay leaf, pounded fine
1 small onion, chopped fine	2 tablespoons butter (or more if needed)
½ stalk celery, chopped fine	
Pinch of thyme, pounded fine	

Place all ingredients in saucepan and stew slowly until tender. Add more butter as needed to prevent burning.

BAKED LOBSTER SAVANNAH
(SERVES 4)

While the origin of Lobster Savannah is unknown, there is evidence beyond its name indicating that its antecedents are indeed along the southeast coast. For instance, in *Charleston Receipts*, a mouth-watering cookbook prepared and published by the Junior League of Charleston, S.C., in 1950, there is an old recipe for a sauce for shrimp, lobster or chicken which is very similar to that for Lobster Savannah. One wonders what wanderer could have brought it to Boston.

2 ounces butter
2 cups sliced mushrooms
1 cup diced green pepper
1 generous tablespoon Spanish paprika
1½ cup sherry wine
Salt and pepper

4 cups cream sauce (page 193)
½ cup diced pimientos
Four 3-pound lobsters, boiled and cooled
Grated Parmesan cheese

The Sauce
Heat butter to melting point in large saucepan, add mushrooms and green pepper. Cook until tender. Add paprika and stir in sherry. Cook until liquid is reduced by ½. Salt and pepper to taste; add cream sauce and pimientos and blend well. Bring to a simmer.

The Lobster
This can be done while vegetables are cooking. Remove claws and knuckles from lobster. Hold lobster with its top side up. With kitchen shears, cut an oval opening in top of shell from tip of tail to base of head. Remove meat from body, claws and knuckles. Cut in large dice. (Discard intestinal vein and stomach—a hard sac near the head—before dicing.) Add meat to

sauce and simmer slowly for 10 minutes. Divide mixture evenly and spoon back into lobster shells. Dust with grated cheese and brown in a 375-degree oven for 15 minutes.

COQUILLE OF LOBSTER SAVANNAH
Place above mixture in scallop shells or ovenproof dishes with a piping of Duchess potatoes (page 184) around the edge, add cheese and brown.

LOBSTER NEWBURG
(SERVES 4)

This rich concoction was first served at Delmonico's in New York after a recipe provided by Charles Delmonico's friend, Ben Wenberg, a sea captain. After a falling out between the two men, Delmonico dropped the dish from his menu. Forced by popular demand to restore it, his revenge took the form of reversing the spelling of the first syllable of Wenberg's name. The second syllable developed into "burg" later.

2 tablespoons butter	1 cup light cream
1½ pounds fresh lobster meat cut in large chunks	1 cup cream sauce (page 193)
1 tablespoon paprika	Salt and pepper
½ cup dry sherry	

Melt butter in saucepan and add lobster meat. Sauté until meat is warmed through. Add paprika and sherry. Continue to cook for 2 minutes. Add fresh cream and cook until mixture is reduced by ¼, add cream sauce and stir gently until thoroughly blended. More or less cream sauce may be used, depending upon thickness desired. Salt and pepper to taste. Serve with toast points or Rice Pilaf (page 185).

CRABMEAT À LA DEWEY
(SERVES 4.)

On May 1, 1898, five days after the declaration of war with Spain, Commodore George Dewey, commander of the Asiatic Squadron based at Hong Kong, destroyed a Spanish fleet in Manila Bay and was immediately the hero of his homeland, provoking the production of sculptures, lithograph portraits, souvenir spoons and miscellaneous memorabilia—as well as Crabmeat à la Dewey, created by the chef at the Maryland Yacht Club.

1 large green pepper	3 tablespoons pimientos
½ pound mushrooms	Salt and pepper
2 tablespoons butter	1½ pounds fresh crabmeat
¾ cup Sauterne wine	Grated Parmesan cheese
2 cups cream sauce (page 193)	

Cut green pepper and mushrooms into julienne (fine strips). Sauté in butter until tender. Add wine and simmer until liquid is reduced by ½. Add cream sauce and pimientos. Season with salt and pepper to taste. Bring to a boil and fold in crabmeat, lower heat to a simmer. Spoon mixture into an ovenproof casserole, top with grated cheese and brown under the broiler. Locke-Ober's serves this with Rice Pilaf (page 185) and green peas.

CRAB LOUIS
(SERVES 6)

Crab Louis was created by the chef of the Olympic Club in Seattle, Washington, around the turn of the century.

Shredded lettuce	Chopped chives
1½ pounds fresh crabmeat	Dressing (see below)
6 hard boiled eggs	

Make beds of shredded lettuce on six salad plates. Pick 1½ pounds fresh crabmeat in big pieces, reserving the claw meat for garnishing. Put a mound of crabmeat on each plate and top it with the claw meat. Rice the eggs and sprinkle them and the chopped chives around the crab.

Dressing

1 cup mayonnaise (page 202)	2 tablespoons chopped green olives
¼ cup French dressing (page 203)	1 teaspoon white horseradish
½ teaspoon tarragon	1 teaspoon Worcestershire sauce
½ cup chili sauce	Salt
	Fresh ground black pepper

Mix all ingredients well and serve on salad.

Variations: add chopped pimiento, chopped pickle relish, or chopped ripe and stuffed olives to the dressing.

BROILED CAPE SCALLOPS WITH BACON
(SERVES 4)

This inspired marriage of scallops and bacon is without any doubt the most popular fish dish with men at lunchtime at Locke-Ober's. In buying scallops, incidentally, it is important to find what should be described as Cape (as on Locke's menu) or bay scallops, which are smaller, sweeter and more tender than the larger sea scallops.

2 pounds fresh or frozen Cape (or bay) scallops— depends on season	1 cup fresh bread crumbs
	1 teaspoon salt
	Fresh ground pepper
¼ cup melted butter	8 strips of bacon

Dry scallops slightly in a paper towel. Mix butter and bread crumbs in a large bowl. Add salt and pepper. Add scallops and mix well. Each scallop should be well covered with the crumbs. Divide scallops on eight metal skewers (two skewers per person) and place under a hot broiler 5 inches from the heat. Turn so all sides are well browned. Cook bacon strips until crisp. Place scallops on four plates, remove skewers, top with bacon and serve with tartar sauce and lemon wedges.

CAPE SCALLOPS SAUTÉ AU SHERRY
(SERVES 4)

2 pounds Cape (or bay) scallops
Flour
Cooking oil

Salt and pepper
¼ pound butter
¼ cup sherry wine
Pinch chopped parsley

Drain scallops and dry them in a kitchen towel. Dredge in flour and shake vigorously to remove all excess flour. In an iron skillet heat ¼ inch of cooking oil almost to the smoking point. Add ½ the scallops and brown lightly—about 5 minutes, do not overcook. Remove from pan, replace cooking oil and cook remaining scallops. Salt and pepper scallops and keep warm. Drain all excess fat from pan and add butter; heat until it turns a light brown. Remove from stove, add sherry and parsley. Pour over scallops and serve.

PLANKED FILLET OF HADDOCK (OR COD), WINTER PLACE

(SERVES 4)

Four 12-ounce haddock fillets, skinned
Flour
½ cup cooking oil
Duchess potatoes (page 184)
4 Little Neck clams on half shell
4 Cape oysters on half shell

¼ cup melted butter
1 cup fresh bread crumbs
1 teaspoon salt
Fresh ground pepper
Juice of ½ lemon
4 strips bacon
2 tablespoons butter
8 thick slices tomato

Dredge fillets in flour. Heat cooking oil in frying pan and cook fillets over moderate heat until done. With a pastry bag pipe a ring of Duchess potatoes (mashed with egg yolk, no cream) onto the outer edge of four 10-inch oval planks (or ovenproof dishes). Bed 1 clam and 1 oyster in Duchess potatoes at opposite ends of each plank. Mix melted butter, bread crumbs, salt, pepper and lemon juice and spoon over clams and oysters. Top each one with ½ piece of bacon and place in a 400-degree oven until bacon is crisp.

Heat butter in saucepan, add tomato slices and cook gently on both sides, about 3 minutes to a side.

Add fillets to planks with tomato slices alongside. Put all back in oven for 2 minutes. Serve very hot.

FINNAN HADDIE DELMONICO
(SERVES 4)

Finnan haddie is smoked haddock named for the Scottish fishing village of Findon. It has long been popular along the New England coast as a way of preserving the haddock catch. Finnan Haddie Delmonico was created at the famous New York Delmonico restaurant which was founded in 1827 and continued to thrive in various locations and under the managership of various Delmonico brothers and sisters until well into the twentieth century.

1½ pounds finnan haddie	2 cups Duchess potatoes
2 cups cream sauce (page 193)	(page 184)
	Grated Parmesan cheese
2 hard boiled eggs, quartered	Salt and pepper

Place finnan haddie in a shallow pan and barely cover with water. Bring to a slow boil and cook for 20 minutes. Drain water from fish and let it cool. Remove all bones, and flake fish into good-sized pieces. Prepare cream sauce and add fish and quartered hard boiled eggs. Salt and pepper to taste. Fold carefully to avoid mashing the flaked fish. Put mixture into a heatproof casserole and surround with a border of Duchess potatoes. Sprinkle top generously with grated fresh Parmesan cheese. Place in a 400-degree oven until top is golden brown.

STEAMED FINNAN HADDIE
(SERVES 1)

Steam a ¾-pound piece of finnan haddie for 15 minutes. Cover generously with melted butter. Serve with lemon wedges and boiled potato.

CURRY OF SHRIMP WITH RICE
(SERVES 4)

28 large raw peeled shrimp	Curry sauce (page 200)
4 ounces butter	Curried rice (see below)
½ cup sherry wine	

Sauté peeled shrimp in butter, add sherry and boil until liquid is reduced by ½, add curry sauce and simmer 5 minutes. Divide curried rice among four individual casseroles. Arrange 7 shrimp on each portion of rice and coat with curry sauce. Serve with the usual curry condiments. Put extra curry sauce on table.

Curried Rice

1 tablespoon butter	¼ cup tomato puree
1 medium onion, diced fine	2 cups chicken stock
1 cup rice	1 teaspoon salt
1½ teaspoons curry powder	

Melt butter in heavy saucepan. Add onion and sauté until transparent. Add rice and cook until butter is absorbed. Add curry powder and tomato puree and stir until well blended. Add chicken stock and salt, cover, and bake in a 350-degree oven for 20 minutes, or until rice is tender.

144

FILLET OF SOLE MARGUERY

(SERVES 4.)

This is a Locke-Ober variation on one of the most famous recipes for sole—created by M. Mangin, Chef, in the old pre-World War II Marguery Restaurant in Paris.

2 pounds sole fillets, divided into 8 pieces	¼ cup lemon juice Salt and pepper
8 large shrimp (15 per pound, peeled raw)	4 ounces butter ⎱ roux ½ cup flour ⎰
8 oysters, shucked	2 cups cream sauce (page 193)
12 mushroom caps	
2 cups fish stock (page 198)	2 egg yolks, beaten
1 cup dry white wine	½ cup unsweetened whipped cream
3 shallots, chopped fine	

Fold sole fillets in half and place in a baking dish with shrimp, oysters and mushrooms. Cover with stock, white wine, shallots and lemon juice. Sprinkle with salt and pepper, cover with oiled paper and poach in a 350-degree oven for 20 minutes. Remove sole fillets and keep hot in an ovenproof casserole. Top with mushroom caps. Reduce stock in which fish was poached to ½, add roux to thicken and simmer for 5 minutes, blending smooth with a whisk. Add cream sauce and egg yolks and bring to a boil. Remove from heat and gently fold in whipped cream. Strain sauce over top of fish and glaze in the oven until golden brown. Serve hot, with *fleurons* (small pastry decorations).

145

BROILED FRESH SCROD (*OR* SCHROD)
(SERVES 4.)

Contrary to popular belief—even in New England where scrod appears most commonly on restaurant menus—there is no such fish. For scrod a Locke-Ober chef prefers to use haddock fillets, although, in fact, almost any white fish will do.

1 cup fresh bread crumbs	Four 12-ounce haddock
¼ cup melted butter	fillets, skin on
Salt and pepper	¼ cup salad oil

Mix bread crumbs and melted butter. Add a pinch of salt and pepper. Brush haddock fillets on both sides with oil. Coat both sides with breadcrumb mixture. Lay on a broiler rack, skin side up. Place in broiler about 5 inches from fire. Broil until skin is blistered and well browned. Turn. Continue to broil until crumbs are a golden brown. Serve with cheese sauce (page 195) and lemon wedges.

MOUSSE OF DOVER SOLE CARDINAL
(SERVES 4)

The Mousse

10 ounces uncooked English   ¾ cup heavy cream
    Sole fillets   2 tablespoons Madeira wine
  3 egg whites

Pass uncooked sole fillets through a very fine grinder three times. Place fish in a round bowl and set bowl in shaved ice. With a wire whisk, beat fish, add the egg whites one by one and continue to beat vigorously. Continue beating and add heavy cream bit by bit; continue with Madeira and beat vigorously until mixture is smooth. Butter generously four *timbales* (drum-shaped ovenproof dishes or pastry crusts in the same shape) and fill about ¾ full with the mousse. Hollow out middle and fill with the following salpicon* of chicken lobster knuckles.

The Filling

5 ounces lobster knuckles   2 tablespoons sherry wine
1 shallot, chopped fine   ½ cup fish velouté (page
1 tablespoon butter   199)

Sauté lobster and shallots in 1 generous tablespoon of butter. Cook until shallots are transparent, add wine and continue to simmer until wine is reduced by ½. Add fish velouté and bring to a boil. Let mixture cool and divide equally into prepared *timbales*. Cover with more sole mousse. Place *timbales* in flat pan and cover bottom of pan with ¾ of an inch of warm water. Bake in a 350-degree oven for about 35 to 40 minutes. Turn mousse out on a serving platter and cover with the following sauce.

* Salpicon: a mixture of one or more diced ingredients bound with a sauce.

The Sauce

1 large truffle, cut in julienne (long strips)

¼ cup sherry wine
Claw meat from 3 medium lobsters, cut in julienne

1 cup of fish velouté (page 199)

6 tablespoons heavy cream
Salt and pepper

Place truffles and wine in saucepan and simmer until wine is reduced by ½; add lobster, hot velouté and simmer. Salt and pepper to taste. Add heavy cream, blend and serve.

Part of the secret of success in life is to eat what you like and let the food fight it out inside.

MARK TWAIN

COQ AU VIN BOURGUIGNONNE (*UNDER GLASS*) '
(SERVES 4)

Two 2½-pound chickens, boned and quartered
1 clove garlic, cut in half and crushed
2 sprigs thyme
1 bay leaf
2 stalks celery, diced
1 carrot, diced
½ pound white onions, diced
1 clove
2 cups red Burgundy wine
4 tablespoons butter
½ pound fresh mushrooms, sliced
2 tablespoons flour
12 black bing cherries with ½ cup juice
Salt and pepper
Chopped parsley

Place cut chicken in a crock. Add garlic, thyme, bay leaf, celery, carrot, onions and the clove. Cover with red wine and marinate for at least 24 hours. Remove chicken and pat dry with a clean towel. Reserve the liquid. Sauté chicken in 2 tablespoons butter until well browned on one side. Turn chicken and add the mushrooms; continue to cook until mushrooms are tender. In another pan melt the remaining 2 tablespoons butter; add flour and stir until well blended. Add liquid remaining in crock, cherries and juice and simmer until mixture reaches the desired thickness (15 minutes). Salt and pepper to taste. Strain this sauce over chicken and mushrooms and simmer very slowly until chicken is cooked, about 30 minutes. Place chicken on shirred egg dishes (or individual casseroles) and cover with sauce and mushrooms. Sprinkle with chopped parsley. Then cover with glass bells and serve.

CHICKEN DIVAN
(SERVES 4)

This dish was the staple and specialty of the elegant Divan Parisienne Restaurant, now extinct, in the old Chatham Hotel in New York where it was served with many flourishes.

1 large bunch broccoli	3 tablespoons sherry wine
4 tablespoons butter	Salt and pepper
4 tablespoons flour	½ cup fresh grated Parmesan
2 cups chicken stock	18 slices cooked chicken
½ cup heavy cream, whipped	

Cook broccoli in boiling salted water for about 10 minutes or until just tender. Drain and keep hot.

Make sauce as follows: Melt butter in a saucepan, blend in flour and gradually add chicken stock, stirring constantly until sauce is thick and smooth. Cook over a low flame for about 10 minutes, stirring frequently. Fold in whipped cream and sherry. Season to taste.

Place the cooked broccoli on a hot ovenproof platter and pour over it ½ the sauce. To the remaining sauce add ¼ cup grated Parmesan. Over the sauce-covered broccoli arrange 18 or so thin slices of cooked chicken. Cover the chicken with the remaining sauce and sprinkle with additional Parmesan. Set the dish under the broiler until the sauce bubbles and is lightly browned.

*The chicken is the usefullest animal there is:
you can eat it before it's born and after it's
dead.*

SOUTHERN FOLK SAYING

BREAST OF CHICKEN SAUTÉ RICHMOND
(*UNDER GLASS*)
(SERVES 4)

6 tablespoons butter	slices, cut to the size of a
4 boned chicken breasts	piece of toast
12 medium-sized mushroom	2 cups cream sauce (page
caps	193)
¾ cup sherry wine	Salt and pepper to taste
¾ cup light cream	4 slices white toast, well
Four ¼-inch-thick ham	done

Heat half of the butter in a large sauté pan, add chicken
breasts, skin side down, and cook until golden brown. Turn
breasts and add mushroom caps. Cook for about 5 minutes,
discard excess fat and add ½ the sherry, ½ the cream, the ham
slices and cream sauce, and a dash of salt and pepper. Cover
and place in a 350-degree oven for about 30 minutes or until
breasts are tender.

Place a slice of well-done toast in each of four shirred egg
dishes or individual ovenproof casseroles. Place ham slices on
top of toast; put chicken breasts on ham and divide mushroom
caps evenly. To sauce remaining in pan add remaining sherry,
cream and butter. Blend well with a wire whisk and simmer
for 2–3 minutes. Strain over chicken. Cover each dish with a
glass bell (*sous cloche*) and place in a hot oven until the glass
is clear of condensation.

CHICKEN POT PIE À LA WINTER PLACE
(SERVES 4)

First Step

Two 3½-pound chickens, cleaned and quartered	3 cups chicken stock
2 stalks celery, chopped	1 small bay leaf
1 large onion, chopped	1½ cups water
	Salt and pepper

Place all ingredients in a large pot. Bring to a boil and simmer slowly for about an hour, or until chicken is well cooked. Remove chicken, cool, remove meat from bones and cut in large strips. Keep remaining stock at a simmer and reduce (boil down) to 1 quart.

Second Step

½ cup butter ⎫ roux	Reserved stock from first
½ cup flour ⎭	step

Melt butter in large saucepan. Blend in flour and cook slowly for 2 to 3 minutes. Keep stirring and do not allow this to brown. With a wire whisk, slowly stir hot stock into roux until well blended. Cover and put in a 275-degree oven for about 45 minutes. Stir occasionally.

Third Step

2 medium carrots, peeled and cut in medium dice	3 stalks celery, cut in medium dice
	2 ounces butter

Place all ingredients in a covered sauté pan and cook very slowly, over low heat, until vegetables are tender, about 25 minutes. Watch carefully for burning. Set aside to cool.

Fourth Step

One-half a 10-ounce pack-   4 small new potatoes
age frozen peas

Undercook the peas and cool in cold water. Boil the potatoes.

Fifth Step

¾ cup light cream   Salt and pepper
1 egg yolk, beaten   Pie dough for 4 top crusts
2 tablespoons butter

Remove velouté (sauce) (second step) from oven. Combine cream and egg yolk and blend; beat into velouté and simmer for 3 to 4 minutes. Strain through a French colander. Stir in butter, salt and pepper to taste, and keep sauce warm. Divide carrot and celery mixture (third step) into four small oval casseroles. Drain peas, add chicken and divide among the casseroles. Add drained potatoes and sauce, cover with your favorite pie crust and bake in a 375-degree oven until crust is done.

ROAST DUCK, SAUCE BIGARADE
(SERVES 4)

2 small ducks, 4½ pounds
each
Salt

Lemon
1 quart Bigarade sauce (page
197)

Place ducks on a rack in a shallow roasting pan. Rub with salt
and lemon. Place in a 350-degree oven for 2 to 2½ hours. Turn
occasionally so they will brown on all sides. Be sure to use a
rack as ducks are very greasy. Remove ducks from roaster and
allow to cool. Split them in half and remove all bones. Place
dressed ducks under the broiler and heat through. Serve with
hot Bigarade sauce. Endive salad goes well (page 180); also
wild rice sautéed with mushrooms.

CASSEROLE OF NATIVE DUCK, TOULOUSAINE
(SERVES 4)

2 five-pound ducks, roasted
10 medium mushrooms,
quartered
1 small onion, chopped
2 shallots, chopped
1 bay leaf

1 tablespoon butter
¼ cup sherry wine
2 cups Bigarade sauce (page
197)
Salt
Pepper

Cube the meat from the ducks and reserve.

Simmer mushrooms, onion, shallots and bay leaf in butter
until tender, remove bay leaf and add cubed duck meat. Add
sherry and sauce, and salt and pepper if needed. Simmer for
10 minutes. Serve with orange sections and wild rice.

FILET MIGNON ROSSINI

(SERVES 4.)

Four 11-ounce tenderloin steaks

4 tablespoons butter

2 shallots, chopped fine

1 cup good domestic claret wine

1 cup brown sauce (page 196)

1 large chicken or medium duck liver

1 tablespoon black brushed truffle, chopped fine

Salt and pepper

4 slices pâté de foie gras

Allow steaks to reach room temperature. Place 1 tablespoon butter in medium saucepan, add shallots and cook slowly until shallots are transparent. Add claret and simmer until wine is reduced by almost ½. Add brown sauce and simmer for ½ hour. Sauté liver in 1 tablespoon of butter, cool, and press through a sieve. Add liver, chopped truffle and 1 tablespoon butter to sauce. Keep hot.

Brush the 4 steaks with melted butter. Sprinkle with salt and pepper and place under a hot broiler. Broil about 10 minutes on each side. Remove from fire and place slice of pâté on top. Put under broiler ½ minute longer and serve with sauce. Parisienne Potatoes (page 184) are recommended with this entrée.

LOCKE-OBER FILET MIGNON, MIRABEAU
(SERVES 4)

Not the traditional Mirabeau garnish, which uses anchovies and black olives, but nevertheless honoring the dining facilities of the Hotel Mirabeau on the Rue de la Paix in Paris which went into bankruptcy during the Depression. The Mirabeau, incidentally, was where the famous Henri Soulé of New York's late lamented Pavillon Restaurant learned the skills of the maitre d'hôtel.

Four 11-ounce tenderloin steaks
12 medium mushroom caps, sautéed
Parisienne Potatoes (page 184)
Tomatoes Provençale (page 179)
Sauce Champignon (page 198)

Place steaks under a hot broiler and cook approximately 10 minutes on each side. Transfer to a serving dish and top each steak with 3 sautéed mushroom caps. Garnish with Parisienne Potatoes and Tomatoes Provençale. Serve with Sauce Champignon.

SLICED FILET OF TENDERLOIN SAUTÉ CHAMPIGNON
(SERVES 4)

Eight ¾-inch slices tenderloin steak

4 tablespoons butter (preferably sweet)

Salt and pepper

Sauce Champignon (page
198)

Have butcher cut 8 slices from the heart of the tenderloin.
Each slice should be about ¾ inch thick. Place in two sauté
pans and sauté in butter until medium rare. Season with salt
and pepper. Arrange slices on serving platter and coat with
Sauce Champignon.

TENDERLOIN À LA STROGANOFF
(SERVES 4.)

The name of this universally popular dish has had such fanciful explanations as a Polish innkeeper's impromptu scrape-together dinner for a czar and a Parisian restaurant's compliment to a Russian ambassador. Actually, despite its operettalike name, its antecedents are probably no more Russian than Russian dressing.

2 pounds lean tenderloin steak	½ cup sherry wine
2 tablespoons butter	2 cups Smitane sauce (page 194)
1½ cups sliced mushrooms	Salt and pepper

Cut beef into long, narrow strips. Place 1 tablespoon of butter and the mushrooms in a saucepan and cook until tender. Add wine and cook until it is reduced by ½. Add Smitane sauce and simmer for 30 minutes.

Place remaining butter in a sauté pan. Heat to smoking point, add tenderloin and sauté until meat is well browned. Add sauce and blend well. Salt and pepper to taste. Place in individual casseroles and serve with buttered noodles.

NEW ENGLAND BOILED DINNER
(SERVES 4.)

One 3 to 4-pound heavy steer New England-style brisket	2 large carrots, split and cut into 2-inch pieces
1 large white cabbage, quartered	12 small silver onions, peeled
	8 small fresh beets
	4 medium Maine potatoes

Place brisket in pot and cover with cold water. Bring to a boil and simmer slowly for about 3 hours, until tender. Remove and keep warm. To the water the brisket was cooked in add the cabbage, carrots and onions and simmer for about ¾ hour, or until vegetables are cooked. Simmer beets in separate pot for about 1 hour or until tender. Simmer potatoes in another pot for about ½ hour, until done. Place slices of hot brisket over cabbage in center of plates. Surround with other cooked vegetables and serve hot.

CASSEROLE OF BEEF CHASSEUR
(SERVES 4)

"Chasseur" is French for hunter, who in gastronomic lore is alleged to be peculiarly susceptible to a method of food preparation combining, mainly, mushrooms and tomatoes, reinforced with shallots and other seasonings.

4 tablespoons butter	2 cups good beef stock, heated to boiling
3 tablespoons olive oil	1½ cups dry red wine
2 pounds lean top round steak, cut in large cubes	Salt and pepper
2 tablespoons Worcestershire sauce	2 shallots, chopped fine
6 tablespoons flour	½ pound sliced mushrooms
	2 medium tomatoes, peeled and chopped fine

Heat 2 tablespoons butter and the oil to frothing point in a large pot and add meat. Cook until all moisture disappears and meat is well browned. Add Worcestershire and simmer for 1 minute. Stir in flour and blend well; cook for 2–3 minutes. Add boiling beef stock and 1 cup of red wine, salt and pepper. Blend and add more water if needed; beef should be just covered. Cook in covered casserole in a 325-degree oven for about 1 to 1½ hours, or until meat is tender. Meanwhile, cook shallots in sauté pan with 2 tablespoons butter until transparent; add mushrooms and cook until tender. Add remaining ½ cup of red wine and reduce liquid by ½, add chopped tomatoes and simmer for 15 to 20 minutes. Remove beef from oven, skim off all excess fat, stir in mushroom mixture and simmer for 5 minutes. Serve with noodles or Rice Pilaf (page 185).

LOCKE-OBER'S SHORT RIBS
(SERVES 4)

Mirepoix (vegetable seasoning for sauce)

½ cup chopped celery	½ cup chopped carrots
½ cup chopped onions	2 tablespoons butter

Simmer the celery, onions and carrots in butter until tender, about 15 minutes.

3 pounds short ribs	2 tablespoons butter ⎱ roux
Flour	2 tablespoons flour ⎰
2 tablespoons cooking oil	1 stalk celery, diced
Mirepoix (see above)	1 carrot, diced
1 cup tomato puree	Salt
⅛ cup sherry wine	Pepper
4 cups beef stock	

Dredge ribs in flour and brown in hot oil. Put in covered casserole with mirepoix, tomato puree, sherry and beef stock. Braise in a 375-degree oven for 1½ hours, until tender. Steam together celery and carrot until tender and reserve. Remove meat and thicken stock with roux. Strain sauce; add salt and pepper to taste and the reserved celery and carrot. Serve over ribs.

KÖNIGSBERGER KLOPS WITH SARDELLAN SAUCE

(SERVES 4)

6 ounces veal	1 egg, beaten
6 ounces pork	¼ cup fine French bread
6 ounces beef	crumbs
½ lemon	Salt
1 small onion, minced	Pepper
2 tablespoons parsley	3 cups beef stock

Grind together the veal, pork, beef, lemon (rind and all) onion and parsley and mix in eggs, crumbs and salt and pepper to taste. Form into medium-sized meatballs and simmer in beef stock for 30 minutes, or until cooked through. Remove the meatballs, keep warm, and use the stock to make the following Sardellan Sauce:

Beef stock (see above)	2 tablespoons capers,
3 tablespoons butter ⎱ roux	chopped
3 tablespoons flour ⎰	5 anchovies, chopped
1 cup cream sauce (page	2 tablespoons parsley,
193)	chopped
½ cup light cream	

Thicken beef stock with roux, add the cream sauce and the light cream, heat and strain. Add capers, anchovies and parsley to the sauce. Serve over the meatballs.

STEAK TARTARE
(SERVES 4)

2 pounds tenderloin steak
1 tablespoon brandy
Lettuce leaves
4 egg yolks
12 anchovy fillets
2 medium onions, chopped fine

2 hard boiled eggs, chopped fine
4 teaspoons capers
Worcestershire sauce (optional)
Salt and pepper

Have the butcher cut from the heart of the loin 2 pounds of very lean tenderloin. With a very sharp French knife chop the beef as fine as you can. Do not use a grinder. Mix in brandy and divide meat equally on four plates covered with lettuce leaves. Make a well in the top of each portion and place egg yolks in the well. Surround yolks with anchovy fillets (3 each). Garnish with chopped onions, chopped eggs and capers. A dash of Worcestershire may be added to each serving if desired. Salt and pepper, and serve with pumpernickel bread.

SCALLOPINI OF VEAL, SMITANE
(SERVES 4)

1½ pounds veal, cut in very thin slices
6 tablespoons butter
½ cup flour
1 ounce dry white wine

1 cup Smitane sauce (page 194)
¼ cup fresh light cream
Salt and pepper

Pound veal slices with a mallet or the flat side of a cleaver until very thin. Dredge slices in 4 tablespoons melted butter and then in the flour. Shake off excess flour. Heat 2 tablespoons butter in sauté pan, add veal and cook to a light brown on both sides. Remove veal from pan and add wine; reduce slightly and add Smitane sauce and cream. Blend well, salt and pepper to taste. Return veal slices to the pan (or put all in a casserole) cover and place in a 350-degree oven for 30 minutes. Transfer veal to a serving platter, add a little more cream and wine to the sauce; strain over veal and serve.

SCHNITZEL NATUR
(SERVES 4)

Four 8-ounce veal cutlets	4 cups sliced fresh mush-rooms
Flour	
Salt and pepper	¾ cup chicken stock
2 tablespoons butter (preferably sweet)	1 tablespoon enrichment butter

Pound veal cutlets well with the flat side of cleaver to about half their original thickness. Dredge slices in flour and season with salt and pepper. In a large sauté pan heat butter to the frothing point, add veal and brown over a brisk fire. Turn cutlets, add mushrooms and continue cooking over a slower fire. When veal is tender all the way through, remove from pan and place on a hot serving platter. Add hot chicken stock to mushrooms and butter and cook until the sauce reduces to a syrupy consistency. Take off the fire. Stir in the enrichment butter and pour mushrooms and sauce over cutlets.

Serve with buttered noodles.

SCHNITZEL HOLSTEIN
(SERVES 4)

Follow instructions for Wiener Schnitzel (page 166), substituting a fried egg for the lemon slice, and surround the yolk with 4 anchovy fillets.

WIENER SCHNITZEL
(SERVES 4)

4 veal cutlets	4 dill pickles
3 eggs	4 lemon slices
½ cup milk	1 cup cold sliced beets
13 slices fresh white bread	4 anchovy rosettes*
Flour	Capers
Salt and pepper	Meunière butter (page
4 tablespoons clarified but-	192)
ter (page 192)	

Have butcher cut slices preferably from the face or top of the round of a small leg of milk-fed veal. With the flat side of a meat cleaver pound veal slices to about half their original thickness. Beat eggs with milk. Trim the crusts from fresh bread and rub bread through a large colander until you have approximately 3 cups of fresh crumbs. Dredge veal slices in flour seasoned with salt and pepper, dip in egg wash and coat generously with the crumbs. Over a medium fire sauté cutlets in clarified butter until both sides are a golden brown. Place on serving platters and garnish each cutlet with sliced beets, sliced dill pickle and one slice of lemon topped with an anchovy rosette filled with capers, and cover generously with meunière butter. Serve with egg noodles topped with Polonaise Butter (page 193).

* Note: To make rosettes, simply roll up a fillet and press to flatten.

VEAL KIDNEYS BRABANÇONNE
(SERVES 8)

Brabançonne refers to Belgium's central province, of which the capital, Brussels, has had a long and distinguished culinary tradition. This dish is usually served with Brussels sprouts or Belgian endive.

8 veal kidneys	1 large bay leaf ⎫
5 tablespoons butter (preferably sweet)	8 sprigs fresh parsley ⎬ bouquet garni
1 clove garlic	1 sprig thyme ⎪
Salt and pepper	2 whole cloves ⎭
½ pound onions, chopped	1 tablespoon brown sugar
2 tablespoons flour	Chopped parsley
2 cups good quality beer	1 tablespoon paprika
	4 slices white toast

Split and wash the kidneys in several changes of cold water. Remove fat, membranes and skin, and pour boiling water over them. Drain and pat dry. Heat butter in an earthenware casserole which has been rubbed with a cut clove of garlic; salt and pepper kidneys and cook until well browned, turning frequently. Add chopped onions and, when they are slightly browned, sprinkle the flour over them and stir until well blended. Gradually pour in the beer, stirring constantly; add the bouquet garni, tied together with kitchen thread, and stir in brown sugar. Cover and simmer very slowly until kidneys are tender, about 20 minutes. Arrange kidneys on a hot platter, taste the sauce for seasoning. Remove the bouquet garni and rub the sauce through a fine-meshed sieve into a saucepan; reheat and pour over kidneys. Dust with parsley and paprika, garnish with toast points.

VEAL PARMIGIANA
(SERVES 4)

4 veal cutlets
3 eggs
½ cup milk
½ cup flour
  Salt and pepper
2 cups bread crumbs
4 tablespoons clarified
  butter (page 192)

3 cups of tomato sauce (page
  199)
8 thin slices Mozzarella
  cheese
4 tablespoons fresh grated
  Parmesan cheese

Have the butcher slice four 7-ounce veal cutlets preferably from the top of the round or bottom round of a veal leg. Pound veal using flat side of a cleaver until half its original thickness.

In a bowl, beat the eggs and milk together. Dredge the cutlets in seasoned flour and then in the egg mixture, then into the fine bread crumbs, pressing down to coat evenly. Heat clarified butter in a sauté pan and add veal. Cook until golden brown on both sides and remove from pan. Wipe out pan and add the tomato sauce (or put it in a baking dish), then return the veal to the pan or the baking dish, if you prefer, and top each cutlet with two slices of Mozzarella. Sprinkle with Parmesan and put into a 450-degree oven until cheese melts. Place on serving platter, add a small portion of sauce to each cutlet and serve with egg noodles topped with Polonaise Butter (page 193).

VEAL CUTLET, BUONNA BOCCA
(SERVES 4.)

4 veal cutlets, ½ pound each

4 thin slices ham

4 thin slices Swiss cheese

4 teaspoons grated Parmesan cheese

½ cup flour

1 egg, beaten with 1 tablespoon water

1 cup bread crumbs combined with 1 cup cracker meal

2 tablespoons cooking oil

2 tablespoons butter

Buonna Bocca Sauce (see below)

Ask your butcher to butterfly the cutlets and pound them flat. On each cutlet lay a slice of ham, a slice of Swiss cheese and 1 teaspoon of grated Parmesan. Fold the cutlets over and secure with toothpicks if needed. Dip each one first in flour, then in egg beaten with water and then in the combined bread crumbs and cracker meal.* Sauté in oil and butter until brown on each side. Finish in a 375-degree oven for 12 minutes. Serve with Buonna Bocca Sauce.

Buonna Bocca Sauce

2 medium onions, diced

½ pound medium mushrooms, quartered

3 shallots, chopped

2 tablespoons butter

1 bay leaf

¼ cup sherry wine

1 whole tomato, chopped

4 cups brown sauce (page 196)

Salt

Pepper

Sauté onions, mushrooms and shallots in the butter until tender. Add bay leaf, sherry and tomato, and reduce liquid until almost gone. Add the brown sauce and let simmer for 20 minutes, stirring constantly to prevent sticking. Remove bay leaf but do not strain the sauce. Salt and pepper to taste.

* A small amount of minced garlic may be added to the crumbs if desired.

CASSEROLE OF VEAL, HUNTER STYLE
(SERVES 4.)

3 pounds stewing veal, cubed

2 tablespoons cooking oil

1 large onion, diced

2 large green peppers, diced

2 cups mushrooms, quartered

1 tablespoon butter

½ cup red wine

2 cups tomato puree

4 cups brown sauce (page 196)

Salt

Pepper

Slowly brown meat in oil, remove and keep warm. Sauté onions, peppers and mushrooms in butter until tender. Add the wine and reduce by half. Mix in the tomato puree and the brown sauce. Return veal to the sauce and simmer slowly for 40 minutes. Salt and pepper to taste. Serve with Rice Pilaf (page 185).

GRILLED SWEETBREADS FIGADOR
(SERVES 4.)

Sweetbread is the euphemism for those glands near the throat and near the heart of calves and lambs. They are most often trimmed and sold in pairs, and two sets are generally sufficient for four diners. Because of their lightness, they are sometimes combined with some other entrée such as chicken or beef in a hearty sauce. Because sweetbreads are unusually perishable, it is important that they be blanched (parboiled) as soon as possible after purchase.

2 large pair sweetbreads	Salt and pepper
Celery leaves	4 tablespoons melted butter
¼ of a lemon	Fresh bread crumbs
A pinch of nutmeg	

Place sweetbreads in cold water for 2–3 hours. Drain and cover with fresh water, a few celery leaves and the lemon quarter and parboil for about 10 minutes. Drain and replace in cold water. Detach the sweetbreads from each other and discard all the skin and sinews. Cut each half into 2 parts lengthwise. Sprinkle with a small pinch of nutmeg and salt and pepper. Dip in melted butter and coat with fine fresh bread crumbs. Place on a broiler rack and broil each side to a golden brown. Place sweetbreads on serving platter and garnish with grilled tomatoes and mushroom caps.

SWEETBREADS EUGÉNIE (*UNDER GLASS*)
(SERVES 4)

The Empress Eugénie (1826–1920) was a lamentable political adviser to her spouse, Napoleon III, but she was a consummate arbiter of fashion and formal entertaining, which probably accounts for her immortality in this contribution to French cuisine.

2 large sweetbreads
2 stalks celery with leaves, chopped
1 carrot, chopped
1 medium onion, chopped
4 tablespoons lemon juice
Flour
6 tablespoons butter (preferably sweet)
12 fresh medium mushroom caps

¾ cup sherry wine
Four ¼-inch-thick ham slices (cut to the size of a piece of toast)
2 cups cream sauce (page 193)
¾ cup light cream
Salt and pepper
4 pieces white toast

Place the sweetbreads in cold water for 2 to 3 hours. Drain and cover with fresh water, add the celery, carrot, onion and lemon juice and parboil for 10 minutes. Remove sweetbreads and cool. Detach them from each other and discard all skin and sinew. Split them in half lengthwise. Dredge in flour. Melt 4 tablespoons butter in a sauté pan and brown sweetbreads on one side. Turn, add mushroom caps and cook until sweetbreads are browned. Drain excess butter and add 4 ounces sherry, the ham slices, cream sauce, fresh cream and salt and pepper to taste. Cover (or put in covered casserole) and place in a 350-degree oven for 10 to 15 minutes.

Place slice of well-done toast in each of four shirred egg dishes or ovenproof individual casseroles. Place ham slices on toast.

Empress Eugénie by Winterhalter.

Divide sweetbreads equally over ham slices and top with mushrooms. To the sauce add the remaining tablespoons sweet butter, a little more fresh cream and the remaining sherry. Blend well and simmer for 2 minutes. Strain sauce equally over sweetbreads. Cover each with a glass bell (*sous cloche*) and place in hot oven until glass is clear of condensation.

BROILED HONEYCOMB TRIPE WITH MUSTARD SAUCE
(SERVES 4)

Two 10-ounce pieces of tripe, not pickled
½ cup chopped celery
½ cup chopped carrots
1 bay leaf
1 tablespoon pickling spice
¼ cup cooking oil
1½ cups fresh bread crumbs
Mustard sauce (page 201)

Simmer tripe, celery, carrots, bay leaf and pickling spice together in 2 cups of water for 2½ hours, until tender. Remove pieces of tripe, and cut each in half through the pocket to make 4 servings. Oil each piece and dredge in bread crumbs. Broil until brown on both sides. Serve with Mustard Sauce and accompany with fried eggplant.

RACK OF LAMB
(SERVES 2)

1 prepared rack of lamb (6 chops)
½ clove garlic
Salt and pepper
2 tablespoons vegetable oil
¾ cup bread crumbs
½ teaspoon rosemary
½ teaspoon marjoram
½ teaspoon thyme
6 teaspoons parsley, chopped
3 tablespoons clarified butter (page 192)

Have the butcher prepare the rack of lamb fully trimmed and ready for roasting. Preheat oven to 450 degrees. Rub lamb with the garlic and sprinkle with salt and pepper. Mince and reserve the garlic. Put the oil into a large sauté pan and heat until almost smoking. Place the lamb, fat side down, in the pan and brown well; turn and brown the other side. Place in oven and roast for 20 minutes.

In a bowl mix thoroughly bread crumbs, herbs, minced garlic and clarified butter. Remove lamb from oven, cover the fat side with breadcrumb mixture and return to oven for 5 minutes, or until brown. Slice the rack into 2 equal servings and accompany with Tomatoes Provençale (page 179), Mushrooms Provençale (page 179), Parisienne Potatoes (page 184) and Mint Sauce (page 200).

THICK ENGLISH LAMB CHOP WITH KIDNEY
(SERVES 4)

4 loin lamb chops	2 tablespoons melted butter
4 lamb kidneys	

Ask butcher for 3-inch-thick boneless loin chops with 3 inches of flank left on. Place a lamb kidney next to the tenderloin or kernel of each chop; wrap flank around chop and secure with a skewer.

Brush chops with melted butter and place under hot broiler. Brown well on one side, turn and brown other side. Move lower in oven and broil for 25 minutes, more or less. The chops should be served medium rare. Accompany with Mint Sauce (page 200).

There is no love sincerer than the love of food.

GEORGE BERNARD SHAW

MUSHROOMS À LA SAM WARD
(SERVES 4.)

Mushrooms à la Sam Ward commemorates the epicurean fancy of the brother of Julia Ward Howe, author of "The Battle Hymn of the Republic." Sam was a colorful bon vivant, raconteur and gastronome, who in Washington political circles in the seventies and eighties was known as the King of the Lobby, an occupation to which he devoted his talents when he was not pursuing more physical pleasures. He was also the inventor of the Sam Ward cocktail for which this is the recipe: "Lay a thin peel of lemon around the inside of a glass. Fill with cracked ice and pour yellow chartreuse over all." Sam said it was his one work of art he hoped might endure but, poor Sam, it has failed to do so.

60 medium mushrooms	2 cups cream sauce (page 193)
½ pound plus 2 tablespoons butter	4 slices white toast
Juice of a lemon	Four ¼-inch-thick slices of ham, heated
Salt and pepper	
1 cup sherry wine	Chopped parsley

Remove and discard stems from the mushrooms and place caps in cold water. Wash well. Cook mushroom caps in ½ pound butter and lemon juice with salt and pepper to taste for about 15 minutes. When tender and still white remove caps with a slotted spoon and set aside. Add sherry to liquid in the pan and reduce by cooking for about 5 minutes.

Add cream sauce to reduced liquid and whip smooth. Strain through a fine strainer, blend in the remaining 2 tablespoons butter and add salt and pepper to taste. Place 4 slices of toast in individual shirred egg dishes (or individual casseroles) and

177

Caricature of Sam Ward for Vanity Fair, *1880, by Sir Leslie Ward—better known as Spy.*

cover each one with a slice of ham. Arrange mushroom caps on ham and heat in oven. Cover caps with sauce and sprinkle with chopped parsley. Cover with a glass bell (*sous cloche*), return to oven and heat until bell clears.

MUSHROOMS PROVENÇALE
(SERVES 4.)

The distinguishing element in so many Provençale dishes is the marked inclusion of garlic, lavishly used in the Provence district of France.

8 large mushrooms	½ clove garlic, minced
8 tablespoons bread crumbs	6 tablespoons clarified but-
¼ bunch parsley, chopped	ter (page 192)

Remove stems from mushroom caps by pulling them out. Do not cut them off.

Mix together well the bread crumbs, parsley, garlic and 4 tablespoons clarified butter. Press the mixture into the mushroom caps and top with a little more clarified butter. Place in a 375-degree oven for 20 minutes, or until brown.

TOMATOES PROVENÇALE
(SERVES 4.)

Follow directions for Mushrooms Provençale (above) using 4 whole tomatoes. Split tomatoes in half horizontally and gently squeeze out excess juice. Press breadcrumb mixture evenly into each half and bake as in mushroom recipe.

BELGIAN ENDIVE AND HEARTS OF PALM VINAIGRETTE
(SERVES 4.)

Boston lettuce	hearts of palm, quartered
4 stalks Belgian endive, cut into large strips	4 small cooked beets, chopped
4 large pieces of canned	Vinaigrette dressing (page 203)

Cover four salad plates with lettuce leaves. Place a bundle of endives in the center of each plate. Surround with palm pieces. Sprinkle the beets over the top and serve with vinaigrette dressing.

BRAISED RED CABBAGE IN WINE
(SERVES 6)

1 large head red cabbage	¼ pound salt pork, chopped
2 onions, chopped	2 cups red wine
1 pound cooked bacon, crumbled	¼ cup brown sugar
	1 cup cider vinegar

Rinse cabbage, drain well and slice. Sauté onions, bacon and salt pork for 10 minutes, and put in a large pot with the cabbage and the wine; add brown sugar and vinegar. Cover and braise in a 375-degree oven approximately 1 hour.

COLE SLAW
(SERVES 6 TO 8)

Sometimes the most puzzling long-held questions yield to the simplest possible answers. Cole slaw, for example. "Cole" is the generic name of the family of plants to which cabbage belongs, and "slaw" derives from the Danish word for salad. The real mystery is who put the two together.

1 large head white cabbage	1 teaspoon salt
½ Spanish onion, shredded fine	½ teaspoon pepper
¼ cup vinegar	3 tablespoons olive oil
2 egg yolks, beaten	1 cup sour cream

Slice cabbage fine, scald 5 minutes in boiling water and drain well. Press out all water, mix with onion and vinegar. Beat egg yolks, salt and pepper together; add oil gradually, beating steadily. Pour over cabbage mixture and stir well. Pour sour cream over all and stir until evenly mixed.

CUCUMBERS À LA DEUTSCH
(SERVES 6)

3 medium-sized cucumbers, sliced	Pinch cayenne pepper
½ teaspoon salt	1 tablespoon lemon juice
1 teaspoon sugar	2 tablespoons vinegar
	1 cup sour cream

Press sliced cucumbers in towel to extract all moisture. Combine salt, sugar and cayenne, mix well and add lemon juice and vinegar, then stir in sour cream. Pour the sauce over the cucumbers.

BOSTON BAKED BEANS
(SERVES 6)

The earliest white settlers of Massachusetts found beans among the food staples of the Indians of the region, and they were quick to appropriate them, partly because beans could be cooked slowly overnight on Saturday and used the next day, when religious laws banned such worldly activity. Later when Sunday cooking was allowed, beans became a traditional New England Saturday night dinner, ideally served with fish cakes and brown bread.

2 cups pea beans	½ pound bacon, chopped
¾ pound salt pork	2 teaspoons onions, chopped fine
½ cup molasses	
2 teaspoons dry mustard	1 teaspoon instant coffee

Soak beans in cold water to cover overnight, then drain. Cover beans with fresh water and cook slowly in a covered pot for 1 hour. Drain and reserve this water. Place ¼ pound salt pork in the bottom of an earthenware bean pot and add beans. Place another ½ pound salt pork midway in the pot and add molasses, mustard, bacon, onions and ½ cup of bean water. Mix gently so as not to break up beans, then cover and bake in a 300-degree oven for 6 hours. Every hour add a little more bean water and stir gently to keep beans moist. During last hour, remove cover and stir in instant coffee.

LOCKE-OBER STUFFING
(SERVES 6 TO 8)

1 medium onion, chopped fine
2 ounces butter
2 loaves stale white bread, crumbed
4 egg yolks

Salt and pepper
2 cups milk
4 tablespoons poultry seasoning

Brown onion in butter, add other ingredients and mix well. Bake in a 350-degree oven for approximately 1 hour.

CANDIED SWEET POTATOES
(SERVES 4)

4 medium sweet potatoes
1 cup maple syrup

1 tablespoon confectioners' sugar

Peel the potatoes and place them in an ovenproof casserole. Pour on the syrup and bake in a 375-degree oven for 1¼ hours, or until soft. Serve hot with some of the syrup and confectioners' sugar on top.

PARISIENNE POTATOES
(SERVES 4)

These small potato balls are a favorite garnish for the serving platter.

2 pounds potatoes, peeled	1 tablespoon fresh chopped
4 tablespoons butter	parsley
Salt and pepper	

With a melon-baller scoop out 1-inch balls from peeled potatoes. Put potato balls in a saucepan, cover with cold water and bring to a boil. Drain and dry on towels. Heat the butter in a heavy pan; add potatoes and cover. Shake pan over medium heat until the potatoes are brown and just tender. Season with salt and pepper. Remove from butter, sprinkle with parsley and place around your serving dish.

Very small new potatoes may also be used in this recipe.

DUCHESS POTATOES
(MAKES 2 CUPS)

These mashed potatoes are often used to decorate a dish or a serving platter.

3 large potatoes, peeled and quartered	5 tablespoons butter
1 egg	Salt and pepper

Simmer potatoes in water until soft. Drain and beat in the egg and 3 tablespoons butter, and season well with salt and pepper. Pipe around the edge of your serving dish with a pastry bag, brush with melted butter and brown under broiler.

RICE PILAF
(SERVES 4.)

1 medium onion, chopped	1 cup rice
4 tablespoons butter	2 cups chicken stock
1 pinch thyme	Salt and pepper

In a saucepan, cook chopped onions in half of the butter until they are transparent. Add thyme and rice, stir well and cook very slowly for 3 minutes. Pour in heated chicken stock, stir and season with salt and pepper. Place in a covered casserole in a 350-degree oven for 20 to 25 minutes. Stir in remaining butter.

RICE ORIENTAL
(SERVES 4.)

1 small onion, chopped	2 cups chicken stock, at the boil
4 tablespoons butter	
1 cup rice	½ cup dried raisins, sautéed in butter
1 teaspoon salt	
½ teaspoon saffron	

In a deep saucepan, brown the onion in 2 tablespoons butter. Add rice, salt and saffron and blend well. Add boiling stock, put in covered casserole and cook in a 350-degree oven for 20 minutes. When done mix in raisins and remaining butter.

This rice dish is good with all curried dishes or with meatballs.

INDIAN PUDDING
(SERVES 4 TO 6)

Next to Lobster Savannah, Indian Pudding may be Locke-Ober's most famous dish. Its smooth texture and elusive flavor linger on the palate and in the memory. This recipe, refined by generations of Locke's chefs, takes all the guesswork out of an old Plymouth Colony "receipt" for the pudding, which went: "Take the morning's milk and throw into it as much cornmeal as you can hold in the palm of your hand. Let the molasses drip in as you sing 'Nearer My God to Thee,' but sing two verses in cold weather."

¼ cup cornmeal
2 cups cold milk
2 cups scalded milk
½ cup molasses
1 teaspoon salt
¼ cup sugar

1 teaspoon cinnamon or ginger or ½ teaspoon of each
4 tablespoons butter
2 tablespoons white rum

Mix the cornmeal with enough of the cold milk to pour easily. Stir until smooth. Add slowly 2 cups scalded milk and cook in the top of a double boiler for 20 minutes, or until thick. Add molasses, salt, sugar, cinnamon (or ginger) and butter. Pour into a buttered pudding dish and pour over the balance of the cold milk and the rum. Set in a pan of hot water and bake 3 hours in a 250-degree oven. Let stand ½ hour before serving. Serve topped with vanilla ice cream. This pudding should be very soft, and should whey, or separate.

One cannot think well, love well, sleep well,
if one has not dined well.

VIRGINIA WOOLF

CHERRIES JUBILEE
(SERVES 4)

48 canned black bing cherries   ¼ cup kirsch
¼ cup cherry juice   ¼ cup brandy
2 teaspoons sugar   4 scoops vanilla ice cream

Place cherries, juice and sugar in a chafing dish. Heat to the boiling point. Add kirsch and brandy, heat for 2 minutes and light mixture with a match. Place 4 scoops of vanilla ice cream in four individual dessert bowls and divide blazing cherries over the ice cream. Macaroons are a great accompaniment to this dish.

187

SULTANA CUPS WITH CLARET SAUCE
(SERVES 4)

This is a variation of the Locke-Ober Sultana Roll with Claret Sauce.

1 quart pistachio ice cream
1 cup stiffly beaten whipped cream
¼ cup walnut meats, chopped

¼ cup maraschino cherries, chopped
¼ cup canned white grapes, chopped
Claret sauce (see below)

Place four medium (6-ounce) souffle cups in the freezer for 3 hours. Take out one at a time. Line bottom and edge with ½-inch thickness of ice cream. Return to freezer. Leave for 2 hours. Mix whipped cream, nuts, cherries and grapes. Fill hollow cavities of molds with mixture and leave in freezer overnight. To serve, turn out onto glass sauce dishes and cover with claret sauce.

Claret Sauce

1 cup simple syrup*   ½ cup claret wine

Mix and pour over sultana cups.

* Simple Syrup: 1/3 cup water and 2/3 cup sugar cooked together until slightly thickened.

BAKED ALASKA
(SERVES 8)

1 sponge cake or pound cake
½ pint vanilla ice cream
½ pint coffee ice cream
½ pint chocolate ice cream
6 egg whites

½ teaspoon cream of tartar
8 tablespoons sugar
¼ cup good quality brandy, heated

Slice 2 pieces of cake about 8 inches long, 4 to 5 inches wide and ½ inch thick. (These pieces will be for the bottom and top.) Place one slice in a flat heatproof dish. Place ice cream on top of cake and mold with a knife to form a square. Place the second piece of cake on top. Cut more slices of cake for the sides and ends. Place in freezer.

Whip egg whites with cream of tartar, gradually adding sugar. When meringue has formed stiff peaks, spread it over the cake with a spatula or use a pastry bag to pipe meringue over cake. When the entire cake is covered (top and sides) bake in a 500-degree oven until it browns, about 30 seconds.

Pour brandy over the Alaska and light. Slice into serving portions.

CRÊPES SUZETTE
(SERVES 4)

Although there are almost as many variations for Crêpes Suzette as there are Crêpes Suzette makers, there seems to be only one clue to their name—that they were originated by Jean Reboux and named for the Princesse de Carnignan, a contemporary of Louis XIV, who was, of course, a Suzette.

The Crêpes

4 eggs
1¼ cups milk
½ cup flour

2 tablespoons melted butter
Oil, for the pan

The Sauce

4 tablespoons butter (preferably sweet)
3 tablespoons granulated sugar
3 oranges

2 lemons
4 tablespoons Grand Marnier
4 tablespoons brandy

In a mixing bowl combine eggs, milk, flour and melted butter. Blend with a wire whisk until smooth, then strain through a sieve.

Heat a 6-inch sauté pan over moderate heat and rub lightly with oil. Using a ladle, quickly pour 1 ounce batter into the pan and tilt the pan to spread the batter as thin as possible. Return to moderate heat for approximately 15 to 20 seconds and flip crêpe to cook on other side. They must cook quickly or they will toughen. Cool on dry towels. This recipe should make 12 crêpes.

The above process is usually done in the kitchen and the finished product done in front of the guests in the dining room.

In a chafing dish with a sterno or alcohol burner, heat the butter until melted; add sugar and cook until caramelized. Grate and reserve the rind of the oranges and lemons. Cut the fruit in half and squeeze juice through cheesecloth or a napkin into the caramelized sugar. Blend until smooth over medium heat. Add grated fruit rinds and Grand Marnier. Add cooked crêpes, one at a time, to simmering sauce, flipping over to heat thoroughly. Fold crêpes into triangle shapes by folding in half twice. Lay side by side on outside edge of the pan and flame with brandy. Serve 3 crêpes per person with 1 ounce sauce from the chafing dish.

ZABAGLIONE
(SERVES 2)

This smooth and piquant Italian custard was probably the precursor of the French Sabayon, which uses Madeira instead of Marsala, and adds cream.

3 egg yolks   ½ cup Marsala wine
¼ cup granulated sugar

Beat the egg yolks and sugar until creamy, add wine and beat in double boiler until thick. Be careful not to beat too long or eggs will curdle. Serve warm in goblets or champagne glasses.

Hunger is the best sauce.

CICERO

CLARIFIED BUTTER

Slowly melt butter (preferably sweet), cool slightly, remove the white solids and save the clear yellow liquid to use in many recipes.

MEUNIÈRE BUTTER

¼ cup clarified butter (see above)
1 tablespoon parsley, chopped

1 teaspoon lemon juice
Salt as needed

Cook butter slowly until light brown. Add parsley and lemon juice and salt if needed.

POLONAISE BUTTER

½ cup dry bread crumbs

4 ounces Meunière butter
(see page 192)

2 hard boiled eggs, chopped
fine

Salt and pepper as needed

Brown the bread crumbs slightly in the butter. Add the eggs and season with salt and pepper if needed. Pour over vegetables or pasta.

CREAM SAUCE
(MAKES 2 CUPS)

4 tablespoons butter

4 tablespoons flour

1 cup milk

1 cup light cream

Pinch salt

In a double boiler, over lightly simmering water, melt butter, stir in flour, blend and let cook for 10 minutes. Heat milk and cream together in a separate pan and stir slowly with a wire whisk bit by bit into flour and butter roux. Add salt and cook slowly for 45 minutes. An alternate method is to place sauce in a covered ovenproof dish and cook in a 275-degree oven for 45 minutes.

For a thinner sauce, more warm milk may be added.

SAUCE MORNAY
(MAKES 1 CUP)

¾ cup cream sauce (page 193)

¼ cup fresh grated Parmesan or Swiss Gruyère cheese

1 egg yolk, beaten

1 tablespoon butter

Blend cream sauce and cheese. Add egg yolk and butter. Blend well and simmer for 5 minutes.

SMITANE SAUCE
(MAKES APPROXIMATELY 2 CUPS)

"Smitane" is the French adjective equivalent for "smetana," the Russian word for sour cream.

1 medium onion, minced

1½ tablespoons butter

½ cup dry white wine

Juice of ½ lemon

1½ cups cream sauce (page 193)

1 cup heavy sour cream

Salt and pepper

Sauté onion in butter until very lightly browned. Add wine and cook slowly until wine is reduced by ½. Add lemon juice, cream sauce and sour cream. Salt and pepper to taste. Simmer *very* slowly for 20 minutes. Do not allow it to boil. Refrigerate if not serving soon and reheat, when needed, in a double boiler or a *bain-marie* [a pot of hot, not boiling, water].

CHEESE SAUCE
(MAKES APPROXIMATELY 1 CUP)

½ cup cream sauce (page 193)
½ cup diced sharp Cheddar cheese
1 dash Worcestershire sauce

1 dash Tabasco
Pinch salt
Dash of yellow food coloring, for color

Warm the cream sauce, add the cheese and melt it in the warm sauce. Add other ingredients and blend. If a thinner sauce is preferred, add a little warm milk.

195

BROWN SAUCE (SAUCE ESPAGNOLE)
(MAKES APPROXIMATELY 1 QUART)

This brown sauce is the base for many derivative sauces, such as Piquante, Madère, Chasseur, Robert, Diable, Bigarade— and it can be kept in the refrigerator for several weeks if carefully sealed, or in the freezer.

	Cooking oil	2	stalks celery, diced
1	beef shin with meat, 2–3 pounds	1	generous pinch thyme
1	small veal knuckle	1	clove garlic, cut in half
	Salt and pepper	8	tablespoons flour
8	tablespoons butter	¾	cup tomato puree
1	large carrot, diced	4	cups beef stock or bouillon
1	bay leaf	2	cups water
1	large onion, diced		

In a large, thick-bottomed pot place a little cooking oil. Place in a 425-degree oven and get it smoking hot. Add beef shin and veal knuckle (have butcher break shin and veal knuckle into medium-sized pieces), salt and pepper, and cook to a golden brown. Add butter and all remaining ingredients except tomato puree and liquids. Blend thoroughly and continue to brown until vegetables are almost tender and flour is a deep brown. In the meantime, mix tomato puree, beef stock and water; bring to a boil. Stir into hot bones and vegetables, and add salt and pepper to taste. Reduce heat to 275 degrees and cook covered for at least 2 hours. Stir frequently. Strain sauce through a medium strainer, place on stove and bring to a slow simmer. Skim off excess fat (or cool overnight and remove fat). Refrigerate until needed.

SAUCE BIGARADE
(MAKES APPROXIMATELY 1 QUART)

This is basically an orange sauce, "bigarade" being French for the bitter orange which was the classic ingredient.

4 oz. butter
1 cup granulated sugar
2 oranges, quartered
1 lemon, quartered
One 8-ounce jar red currant jelly
1½ cup orange juice
1½ cup brown sauce (page 196)
¼ cup cider vinegar
Rind of 1 orange, cut into julienne
Rind of 1 lemon, cut into julienne
3 teaspoons sugar
½ cup sherry wine

Place butter and sugar in a saucepan and cook until the sugar caramelizes to a medium brown. Add quartered oranges, lemon and currant jelly. Stir until well blended and simmer for 5 to 7 minutes. Add orange juice, brown sauce and vinegar and simmer slowly for 30 minutes; strain through a fine strainer.

Cover the orange and lemon rinds with cold water and boil slowly for 10 minutes. Drain off water and add sugar and wine; simmer for 5 minutes and add to sauce.

197

SAUCE CHAMPIGNON
(MAKES ABOUT 1 CUP)

1 tablespoon butter
1 shallot, chopped fine
1 cup fresh mushrooms,
   sliced

½ cup dry red wine
1 cup brown sauce (page
   196), hot

Place butter, shallots and mushrooms in a saucepan. Cook slowly until all liquid from mushrooms disappears. Add wine and continue to simmer until wine is reduced by ½. Stir in hot brown sauce, and simmer for 30 to 40 minutes.

FISH STOCK
(MAKES APPROXIMATELY 1 QUART)

1 large onion, diced
1 stalk celery, chopped
1 ounce butter
2 pounds fish bones and
   trimmings

Juice of ½ lemon
1 cup dry white wine
Salt and pepper
1 quart water

In a medium pot, cook onion and celery in butter until transparent. Add fish bones and trimmings, lemon juice and wine, salt and pepper. Cook until wine is reduced by ½, then add water. Bring to a boil and simmer for one hour. Strain through a fine strainer. Use at once or freeze until needed.

FISH VELOUTÉ
(MAKES APPROXIMATELY 1 QUART)

4 ounces butter
½ cup flour

1 quart fish stock (page
  198)
1 ounce enrichment butter

Melt butter and stir in flour. Cook for 10 minutes on low fire.
Do not brown. With a wire whisk beat in hot fish stock and
blend. Cook over a very low fire for 45 minutes.

Strain through fine strainer and add 1 more ounce butter.

TOMATO SAUCE
(MAKES 1½ QUARTS)

1 onion, diced
2 carrots, diced
1 clove of garlic, chopped
2 ham hocks or a small ham
  bone
½ cup bacon fat
4 tablespoons flour
4 cups whole canned toma-
  toes, core removed

2 cups tomato puree
2 cups chicken stock
3 teaspoons sugar
2 bay leaves
1 teaspoon thyme
1 teaspoon oregano
  Salt and pepper

Cook onions, carrots and garlic with ham hocks in bacon fat
until vegetables are soft. Remove ham hocks and add flour;
cook until flour starts to brown. Add tomatoes, puree and
stock; return ham hocks to mixture. Add sugar, bay leaves,
thyme and oregano and simmer for 2½ hours over low heat.
Salt and pepper to taste. Remove bones and bay leaves and
strain sauce through a fine sieve.

MINT SAUCE
(MAKES APPROXIMATELY 1 QUART)

2 bunches fresh mint	¼ cup cider vinegar
6 tablespoons granulated sugar	4 cups water
	6 tablespoons mint jelly

Remove stems from mint and chop leaves very fine with a sharp knife. When chopping, add 4 tablespoons sugar to leaves to prevent them from turning black. Place in saucepan and add vinegar, water, remainder of sugar and the mint jelly. Let simmer for 1 hour, then cool.

CURRY SAUCE
(MAKES APPROXIMATELY 1 QUART)

6 tablespoons butter	6 tablespoons flour
1 apple, chopped	4 cups chicken stock
1 onion, chopped	½ cup light cream
1 stalk celery, chopped	Salt and pepper
2½ teaspoons curry powder	

Melt butter in heavy saucepan, add apple, onion and celery and braise lightly until tender. Add curry powder and cook for 5 minutes over low heat. Add flour and blend to a smooth paste. Cook over low heat for 5 minutes and add hot chicken stock. Stir until smooth and thickened. Let sauce simmer slowly for 30 minutes and strain. Add cream and salt and pepper to taste. Return to fire and bring to a boil. Remove and keep warm.

MUSTARD SAUCE
(MAKES 4 CUPS)

4 cups brown sauce (page
  196)
½ cup prepared mustard
¼ cup sherry wine

Dash Worcestershire sauce
Dash Tabasco
Salt if needed

Mix all ingredients except the salt in a saucepan, bring to a boil and salt to taste. Strain.

HOLLANDAISE SAUCE
(MAKES APPROXIMATELY 2 CUPS)

1 pound butter
6 egg yolks
3 tablespoons water

3 tablespoons lemon juice
Pinch salt
Dash pepper

Place butter in saucepan and melt very slowly. Allow to sit for 15 minutes so solids will settle to bottom of pan. Save yellow liquid at top and discard sediment. In a stainless steel bowl place egg yolks, water, lemon juice, salt and pepper. Beat with a wire whisk. In a shallow saucepan heat 2 inches of water to a very slow simmer; place bowl in the hot water and beat mixture until it thickens. Remove from hot water and slowly beat in melted butter. This sauce must be used fairly soon. Do not reheat or it will separate.

LOCKE-OBER MAYONNAISE
(MAKES APPROXIMATELY 4 CUPS)

It seems to be a favorite story that "La Sauce Mahonnaise" was conceived by the chef of the Duc de Richelieu to help celebrate the French defeat of the British forces defending Fort Mahon on Minorca in 1756.

Now it is the theory of Roy Andries de Groot, author of *Feasts for All Seasons*, that from that invention it was a logical gastronomic progression to assume that if egg yolks could thicken olive oil, they could also be used to thicken the butter which the French had discovered the Dutch melted and poured advantageously over all kinds of fish "a la Hollandaise." So Hollandaise Sauce came into being (page 201).

8 egg yolks
Salt to taste
2 cups olive oil
1 cup chicken fat
4 tablespoons fresh lemon juice
4 tablespoons white vinegar
2 teaspoons sugar
Cool water if necessary to thin

Place egg yolks in a bowl, add all ingredients except olive oil and beat vigorously with a whisk or rotary beater until well blended. Add oil drop by drop, beating constantly until mixture thickens. If too thick, thin with cool water.

LOCKE-OBER FRENCH DRESSING
(MAKES 3 CUPS)

2 teaspoons salt
½ teaspoon paprika
1 teaspoon dry mustard
1 teaspoon white pepper

2 tablespoons fresh lemon
  juice
¾ cup cider vinegar
1 clove garlic, crushed
2¼ cups olive oil

Place all ingredients except oil in a quart bottle. Shake vigorously until well mixed. Add oil. Cap and let stand for 48 hours. This mixture must be shaken well every time it is served.

LOCKE-OBER VINAIGRETTE DRESSING
(MAKES APPROXIMATELY 1 CUP)

¾ cup Locke-Ober French
  dressing (above)
1 tablespoon pimientos,
  chopped fine
1 tablespoon fresh, chopped
  green pepper

½ tablespoon chopped
  parsley
½ tablespoon chopped
  scallions

Shake all ingredients together in a pint jar.

ROQUEFORT CHEESE DRESSING
(MAKES 1 GENEROUS CUP)

¾ cup Locke-Ober French   ½ cup Roquefort cheese (*not*
    dressing (page 203)   blue cheese)

This makes a fairly thick and hefty dressing. Add more French
dressing to make it thinner.

*I look upon it, that he who does not mind his
belly will hardly mind anything else.*

SAMUEL JOHNSON

RECIPE PAGE NUMBERS

205

The authors live with their two children in Milton, Massachusetts, a suburb of Boston and not too remote from their favorite restaurant. Ned Bradford is a Senior Editor at Little, Brown and Company; his previous book is the one-volume edition of *Battles and Leaders of the Civil War*. Pamela Bradford has worked for two book publishers and a national literary magazine in New York and Boston.